THE
POETRY OF
H. P. LOVECRAFT

By

H. P. LOVECRAFT

INCLUDING THE ESSAYS
The Allowable Rhyme
&
Metrical Regularity

Read & Co.

Copyright © 2020 Ragged Hand

This edition is published by Ragged Hand,
an imprint of Read & Co.

British Library Cataloguing-in-Publication Data
A catalogue record for this book is available
from the British Library.

Read & Co. is part of Read Books Ltd.
For more information visit
www.readandcobooks.co.uk

To
HOWARD PHILLIPS LOVECRAFT

Essayist, Poet &
Master-writer of the Weird
1890-1937

He lived—and now is dead beyond all knowing
Of life and death: the vast and formless scheme
Behind the face of nature ever showing
Has swallowed up the dreamer and the dream.
But brief the hour he had upon the stream
Of timeless time from past to future flowing
To lift his sail and catch the luminous gleam
Of stars that marked his coming and his going
Before he vanished: yet the brilliant wake
His passing left is vivid on the tide
And for the countless centuries will abide:
The genius that no death can ever take
Crowns him immortal, though a man has died.

FRANCIS FLAGG
(*George Henry Weiss*)

CONTENTS

THE POETRY OF H. P. LOVECRAFT

5

6

7

H. P. LOVECRAFT

Howard Phillips Lovecraft was born in 1890 in Rhode Island, USA. Although a sickly boy, Lovecraft began writing at a very young age, quickly developing a deep and abiding interest in science. At just sixteen he was writing a monthly astronomy column for his local newspaper. However, in 1908, Lovecraft suffered a nervous breakdown and failed to get into university, sparking a period of five years in which he all but vanished.

In 1913, Lovecraft was invited to join the UAPA (United Amateur Press Association)—a development which re-invigorated his writing. In 1917, he began to focus on fiction, producing such well-known early stories as *Dagon* and *A Reminiscence of Dr. Samuel Johnson*. In 1924, Lovecraft married and moved to New York, but he disliked life there intensely, and struggled to find work. A few years later, penniless and now divorced, he returned to Rhode Island. It was here, during the last decade of his life, that Lovecraft produced the vast majority of his best-known fiction, including *The Dunwich Horror, The Shadow over Innsmouth, The Thing on the Doorstep* and arguably his most famous story, *The Call of Cthulhu*. Having suffered from cancer of the small intestine for more than a year, Lovecraft died in March of 1937.

THE ALLOWABLE RHYME

By H. P. Lovecraft

"Sed ubi plura nitent in carmine, non ego paucis
Offendar maculis."

— HORACE

The poetical tendency of the present and of the preceding century has been divided in a manner singularly curious. One loud and conspicuous faction of bards, giving way to the corrupt influences of a decaying general culture, seems to have abandoned all the proprieties of versification and reason in its mad scramble after sensational novelty; whilst the other and quieter school, constituting a more logical evolution from the poesy of the Georgian period, demands an accuracy of rhyme and metre unknown even to the polished artists of the age of Pope. The rational contemporary disciple of the Nine, justly ignoring the dissonant shrieks of the radicals, is therefore confronted with a grave choice of technique. May he retain the liberties of imperfect or "allowable" rhyming which were enjoyed by his ancestors, or must he conform to the new ideals of perfection evolved during the past century? The writer of this article is frankly an archaist in verse. He has not scrupled to rhyme "toss'd" with "coast", "come" with "Rome", or "home" with "gloom" in his very latest published efforts, thereby proclaiming his maintenance of the old-fashioned poets as models; but sound modern criticism, proceeding from Mr. Rheinhart Kleiner and from other sources which must needs command respect, has impelled him here to rehearse the question for public benefit, and particularly to present his own side, attempting to justify his adherence to the style of two centuries ago. The earliest English attempts at rhyming probably included words whose agreement is so slight that it deserves the name of mere "assonance" rather than that of actual rhyme. Thus in the original ballad of "Chevy-Chase", we encounter "King" and "within" supposedly rhymed, whilst in the similar "Battle of Otterbourne" we behold "long" rhymed with "down", "ground" with "Agurstonne", and "name" with "again". In the ballad of "Sir Patrick Spense", "morn" and "storm", and "deep" and "feet" are rhymed. But the infelicities were obviously the result not of artistic negligence, but of plebeian ignorance, since the old ballads were undoubtedly the careless products of a peasant minstrelsy. In Chaucer, a poet of the Court, the allowable rhyme is but infrequently discovered, hence we may assume that the original ideal in English verse was the perfect rhyming sound. Spenser uses allowable rhymes, giving in one of his characteristic stanzas the three distinct sounds of "Lord", "ador'd", and "word", all supposed to rhyme; but of his pronunciation we know little, and may justly guess that to the ears of his contemporaries the sounds were not conspicuously different. Ben Jonson's employment of imperfect rhyming was much like Spenser's; moderate, and partially to be excused on account of a chaotic pronunciation. The better poets of the Restoration were also sparing of allowable rhymes; Cowley, Waller, Marvell, and many others being quite regular in this respect. It was therefore upon a world unprepared that Samuel Butler burst forth with his immortal "Hudibras", whose comical familiarity of diction is in grotesqueness surpassed only by its clever licentiousness of rhyming. Butler's well-known double rhymes are of necessity forced and inexact, and in ordinary single rhymes he seems to have had no more regard for precision. "Vow'd" and "would", "talisman" and "slain", "restores" and "devours" are a few specimens selected at random. Close after Butler came John Oldham, a satirist whose force and brilliancy gained him universal praise, and whose enormous crudity both in rhyme and in metre was forgotten amidst the splendour of his attacks. Oldham was almost absolutely ungoverned by the demands of the ear, and perpetrated such atrocious rhymes as "heads" and "besides", "devise" and "this", "again" and "sin", "tool" and "foul", "end" and "design'd", and even "prays" and "cause". The glorious Dryden, refiner and purifier of English verse, did less for rhyme than he did for metre. Though nowhere attaining the extravagances of his friend Oldham, he lent the sanction of his great authority to rhymes which Dr. Johnson admits are "open to objection". But one vast difference betwixt Dryden and his loose predecessors must be observed. Dryden had so far improved metrical cadence, that the final syllables of heroic couplets stood out in especial eminence, displaying and emphasising every possible similarity of sound; that is, lending to sounds in the first place approximately similar, the added similarity caused by the new prominence of their perfectly corresponding positions in their respective lines. It were needless to dwell upon the rhetorical polish of the age immediately succeeding Dryden's. So far as English versification is concerned, Pope was the world, and all the world was Pope. Dryden had founded a new school of verse, but the development and ultimate perfection of this art remained for the sickly lad who before the age of twelve begged to be taken to Will's Coffee-House, that he might obtain one personal view of the aged Dryden, his idol and model. Delicately attuned to the subtlest harmonies of poetical construction, Alexander Pope brought English prosody to its zenith, and still stands alone on the heights. Yet he, exquisite master of verse that he was, frowned not upon imperfect rhymes, provided they were set in faultless metre. Though most of his allowable rhymes are merely variations in the breadth and nature of vowel sounds, he in one instance departs far enough from rigid perfection to rhyme the words "vice" and "destroys". Yet who can take offence? The unvarying ebb and flow of the refined metrical impulse conceals and condones all else. Every argument by which English blank verse or Spanish assonant verse is sustained, may with greater force be applied to the allowable rhyme. Metre is the real essential of poetical technique, and when two sounds of substantial resemblance are so placed that one follows the other in a certain measured relation, the normal ear cannot without cavilling find fault with a slight want of identity in the respective dominant vowels. The rhyming of a long vowel with a short one is common in all the Georgian poets, and when well recited cannot but be overlooked amidst the general flow of the verse; as, for instance, the following from Pope:

> "But thinks, admitted to that equal SKY,
> His faithful dog shall bear him COMPANY."

Of like nature is the rhyming of actually different vowels whose sounds are, when pronounced in animated oration, by no means dissimilar. Out of verse, such words as "join" and "line" are quite unlike, but Pope well rhymes them when he writes:

> "While expletives their feeble aid do JOIN,
> And ten low words oft creep in one dull LINE."

It is the final consonantal sound in rhyming which can never vary. This, above all else, gives the desired similarity. Syllables which agree in vowels but not in final consonants are not rhymes at all, but simply assonants. Yet such is the inconsistent carelessness of the average modern writer, that he often uses these mere assonants to a greater extent than his fathers ever employed actually allowable rhymes. The writer, in his critical duties, has more than once been forced to point out the attempted rhyming of such words as "fame" and "lane", "task" and "glass", or "feels" and "yields", and in view of these impossible combinations he cannot blame himself very seriously for rhyming "art" and "shot" in the March *Conservative;* for this pair of words have at least identical consonants at the end. That allowable rhymes have real advantages of a positive sort is an opinion by no means lightly to be denied. The monotony of a long heroic poem may often be pleasantly relieved by judicious interruptions in the perfect succession of rhymes, just as the metre may sometimes be adorned with occasional triplets and Alexandrines. Another advantage is the greater latitude allowed for the expression of thought. How numerous are the writers who, from restriction to perfect rhyming, are frequently compelled to abandon a neat epigram or brilliant antithesis, which allowable rhyme would easily permit, or else to introduce a dull expletive merely to supply a desired rhyme! But a return to historical considerations shews us only too clearly the logical trend of taste, and the reason Mr. Kleiner's demand for absolute perfection is no idle cry. In Oliver Goldsmith there arose one who, though retaining the familiar classical diction of Pope, yet advanced further still toward what he deemed ideal polish by virtually abandoning the allowable rhyme. In unvaried exactitude run the couplets of "The Traveller" and of "The Deserted Village", and none can deny to them a certain urbanity which pleases the critical ear. With but little less precision are moulded the simple rhymes of Cowper, whilst the pompous Erasmus Darwin likewise shews more attention to identity of sound than do the Queen Anne bards. Gifford's translations of Juvenal and Persius shew to an almost equal degree the tendency of the age, and Campbell, Crabbe, Wordsworth, Byron, Keats, and Thomas Moore are all inclined to refrain from the liberties practiced by those of former times. To deny the importance of such a widespread change of technique is fruitless, for its existence argues for its naturalness. The best critics of the nineteenth and twentieth centuries demand perfect rhyming, and no aspirant for fame can afford to depart from a standard so universal. It is evidently the true goal of the English, as well as of the French bard; the goal from which we were but temporarily deflected during the preceding age. But exceptions should and must be made in the case of a few who have somehow absorbed the atmosphere of other days, and who long in their hearts for the stately sound of the old classic cadences. Well may their predilection for imperfect rhyming be discouraged to a limited extent, but to chain them wholly to modern rules would be barbarous. Every individual mind demands a certain freedom of expression, and the man who cannot express himself satisfactorily without the stimulation derived from the spirited mode of two centuries ago should certainly be permitted to follow without undue restraint a practice at once so harmless, so free from essential error, and so sanctioned by precedent, as that of employing in his poetical compositions the smooth and inoffensive allowable rhyme.

FIRST PUBLISHED IN
July, 1915

METRICAL REGULARITY

By H. P. Lovecraft

Of the various forms of decadence manifest in the poetical art of the present age, none strikes more harshly on our sensibilities than the alarming decline in that harmonious regularity of metre which adorned the poetry of our immediate ancestors.

That metre itself forms an essential part of all true poetry is a principle which not even the assertions of an Aristotle or the pronouncements of a Plato can disestablish. As old a critic as Dionysius of Halicarnassus and as modern a philosopher as Hegel have each affirmed that versification in poetry is not alone a necessary attribute, but the very foundation as well; Hegel, indeed, placing metre above metaphorical imagination as the essence of all poetic creation.

Science can likewise trace the metrical instinct from the very infancy of mankind, or even beyond, to the pre-human age of the apes. Nature is in itself an unending succession of regular impulses. The steady recurrence of the seasons and of the moonlight, the coming and going of the day, the ebb and flow of the tides, the beating of the heart and pulses, the tread of the feet in walking, and countless other phenomena of like regularity, have all combined to inculcate in the human brain a rhythmic sense which is as manifest in the most uncultivated, as in the most polished of peoples. Metre, therefore, is no such false artifice as most exponents of radicalism would have us believe, but is instead a natural and inevitable embellishment to poesy, which succeeding ages should develop and refine, rather than

17

maim or destroy.

Like other instincts, the metric sense has taken on different aspects among different races. Savages shew it in its simplest form while dancing to the sound of primitive drums; barbarians display it in their religious and other chantings; civilised peoples utilise it for their formal poetry, either as measured quantity, like that of Greek and Roman verse, or as measured accentual stress, like that of our own English verse. Precision of metre is thus no mere display of meretricious ornament, but a logical evolution from eminently natural sources.

It is the contention of the ultra-modern poet, as enunciated by Mrs. J. W. Renshaw in her recent article on "The Autocracy of Art" (*The Looking Glass* for May), that the truly inspired bard must chant forth his feelings independently of form or language, permitting each changing impulse to alter the rhythm of his lay, and blindly resigning his reason to the "fine frenzy" of his mood. This contention is of course founded upon the assumption that poetry is super-intellectual; the expression of a "soul" which outranks the mind and its precepts. Now while avoiding the impeachment of this dubious theory, we must needs remark, that the laws of Nature cannot so easily be outdistanced. However much true poesy may overtop the produce of the brain, it must still be affected by natural laws, which are universal and inevitable. Wherefore it is possible for the critic to assume the attitude of the scientist, and to perceive the various clearly defined natural forms through which the emotions seek expressions. Indeed, we feel even unconsciously the fitness of certain types of metre for certain types of thought, and in perusing a crude or irregular poem are often abruptly repelled by the unwarranted variations made by the bard, either through his ignorance or his perverted taste. We are naturally shocked at the clothing of a grave subject in anapaestic metre, or the treatment of a long and lofty theme in short, choppy lines. This latter defect is what repels us so much from Conington's really scholarly translation of the Aeneid.

What the radicals so wantonly disregard in their eccentric performances is unity of thought. Amidst their wildly repeated leaps from one rough metre to another, they ignore the underlying uniformity of each of their poems. Scene may change; atmosphere may vary; yet one poem cannot but carry one definite message, and to suit this ultimate and fundamental message must one metre be selected and sustained. To accommodate the minor inequalities of tone in a poem, one regular metre will amply lend itself to diversity. Our chief, but now annoyingly neglected measure, the heroic couplet, is capable of taking on infinite shades of expression by the right selection and sequence of words, and by the proper placing of the caesura or pause in each line. Dr. Blair, in his 38th lecture, explains and illustrates with admirable perspicuity the importance of the caesura's location in varying the flow of heroic verse. It is also possible to lend variety to a poem by using very judiciously occasional feet of a metre different from that of the body of the work. This is generally done without disturbing the syllabification, and it in no way impairs or obscures the dominant measure.

Most amusing of all the claims of the radical is the assertion that true poetic fervour can never be confined to regular metre; that the wild-eyed, long-haired rider of Pegasus must inflict upon a suffering public in unaltered form the vague conceptions which flit in noble chaos through his exalted soul. While it is perfectly obvious that the hour of rare inspiration must be improved without the hindrance of grammars or rhyming dictionaries, it is no less obvious that the succeeding hour of calmer contemplation may very profitably be devoted to amendment and polishing. The "language of the heart" must be clarified and made intelligible to other hearts, else its purport will forever be confined to its creator. If natural laws of metrical construction be wilfully set aside, the reader's attention will be distracted from the soul of the poem to its uncouth and ill-fitting dress. The more nearly perfect the metre, the less conspicuous its presence; hence if the poet desires supreme consideration for his matter, he should make his verses so smooth that the sense may never be interrupted.

The ill effect of metrical laxity on the younger generation of poets is enormous. These latest suitors of the Muse, not yet sufficiently trained to distinguish between their own artless crudities and the cultivated monstrosities of the educated but radical bard, come to regard with distrust the orthodox critics, and to believe that no grammatical, rhetorical, or metrical skill is necessary to their own development. The result cannot but be a race of churlish, cacophonous hybrids, whose amorphous outcries will waver uncertainly betwixt prose and verse, absorbing the vices of both and the virtues of neither.

When proper consideration shall be taken of the perfect naturalness of polished metre, a wholesome reaction against the present chaos must inevitably occur; so that the few remaining disciples of conservatism and good taste may justly entertain one last, lingering hope of hearing from modern lyres the stately heroics of Pope, the majestic blank verse of Thomson, the terse octosyllabics of Swift, the sonorous quatrains of Gray, and the lively anapaests of Sheridan and Moore.

FIRST PUBLISHED IN
The Conservative, 1915

THE
POETRY OF
H. P. LOVECRAFT

A COLLECTION

ODE TO
SELENE OR DIANA

Immortal Moon, in maiden splendour shine.
Dispense thy beams, divine *Latona's* child.
Thy silver rays all grosser things define,
And hide harsh truth in sweet illusion mild.

In thy soft light, the city of unrest
That stands so squalid in thy brother's glare
Throws off its habit, and in silence blest
Becomes a vision, sparkling bright and fair.

The modern world, with all it's care & pain,
The smoky streets, the hideous clanging mills,
Face 'neath thy beams, *Selene*, and again
We dream like shepherds on *Chaldæa's* hills.

Take heed, *Diana*, of my humble plea.
Convey me where my happiness may last.
Draw me against the tide of time's rough sea
And let my sprirt rest amid the past.

FIRST PUBLISHED IN
The Tryout, April 1919

ON RECEIVING
A PICTURE OF SWANS

With pensive grace the melancholy Swan
Mourns o'er the tomb of luckless Phaëton;
On grassy banks the weeping poplars wave,
And guard with tender care the wat'ry grave.
Would that I might, should I too proudly claim
An Heav'nly parent, or a Godlike fame,
When flown too high, and dash'd to depths below,
Receive such tribute as a Cygnus' woe!
The faithful bird, that dumbly floats along,
Sighs all the deeper for his want of song.

FIRST PUBLISHED IN
The Conservative, January 1916

TO THE OLD
PAGAN RELIGION

Olympian gods! How can I let ye go
And pin my faith to this new *Christian* creed?
Can I resign the deities I know
For him who on a cross for man did bleed?

How in my weakness can my hopes depend
On one lone God, though mighty be his pow'r?
Why can *Jove's* host no more assistance lend,
To soothe my pain, and cheer my troubled hour?

Are there no Dryads on these wooded mounts
O'er which I oft in desolation roam?
Are there no Naiads in these crystal founts?
Nor Nereids upon the Ocean foam?

Fast spreads the new; the older faith declines.
The name of *Christ* resounds upon the air.
But my wrack'd soul in solitude repines
And gives the Gods their last-receivèd pray'r.

FIRST PUBLISHED IN
The Tryout, April 1919

UNDA

OR,
THE BRIDE OF THE SEA

Respectfully
Dedicated with Permission to
Maurice Winter Moe, Esq.
A Dull, Dark, Drear, Dactylic Delirium
in Sixteen Silly, Senseless, Sickly Stanzas

"Ego, canus, lunam cano."
— Maevius Bavianus

Black loom the crags of the uplands behind me;
Dark are the sands of the far-stretching shore.
Dim are the pathways and rocks that remind me
Sadly of years in the lost nevermore.

Soft laps the ocean on wave-polish'd boulder;
Sweet is the sound and familiar to me.
Here, with her head gently bent to my shoulder,
Walk'd I with Unda, the Bride of the Sea.

Bright was the morn of my youth when I met her,
Sweet as the breeze that blew in o'er the brine.
Swift was I captur'd in Love's strongest fetter,
Glad to be hers, and she glad to be mine.

Never a question ask'd I where she wander'd,
Never a question ask'd she of my birth:
Happy as children, we thought not nor ponder'd,
Glad with the bounty of ocean and earth.

Once when the moonlight play'd soft 'mid the billows,
High on the cliff o'er the waters we stood,
Bound was her hair with a garland of willows,
Pluck'd by the fount in the bird-haunted wood.

Strangely she gaz'd on the surges beneath her,
Charm'd by the sound or entranc'd by the light.
Then did the waves a wild aspect bequeath her,
Stern as the ocean and weird as the night.

Coldly she left me, astonish'd and weeping,
Standing alone 'mid the regions she bless'd:
Down, ever downward, half gliding, half creeping,
Stole the sweet Unda in oceanward quest.

Calm grew the sea, and tumultuous beating
Turn'd to a ripple, as Unda the fair
Trod the wet sands in affectionate greeting,
Beckon'd to me, and no longer was there!

Long did I pace by the banks where she vanish'd:
High climb'd the moon, and descended again.
Grey broke the dawn till the sad night was banish'd,
Still ach'd my soul with its infinite pain.

All the wide world have I search'd for my darling,
Scour'd the far deserts and sail'd distant seas.
Once on the wave while the tempest was snarling,
Flash'd a fair face that brought quiet and ease.

Ever in restlessness onward I stumble,
Seeking and pining, scarce heeding my way.
Now have I stray'd where the wide waters rumble,
Back to the scene of the lost yesterday.

Lo! the red moon from the ocean's low hazes
Rises in ominous grandeur to view.
Strange is its face as my tortur'd eye gazes
O'er the vast reaches of sparkle and blue.

Straight from the moon to the shore where I'm sighing
Grows a bright bridge, made of wavelets and beams.
Frail may it be, yet how simple the trying;
Wand'ring from earth to the orb of sweet dreams.

What is yon face in the moonlight appearing;
Have I at last found the maiden that fled?
Out on the beam-bridge my footsteps are nearing
Her whose sweet beckoning hastens my tread.

Currents surround me, and drowsily swaying,
Far on the moon-path I seek the sweet face.
Eagerly hasting, half panting, half praying,
Forward I reach for the vision of grace.

Murmuring waters about me are closing,
Soft the sweet vision advances to me:
Done are my trials; my heart is reposing
Safe with my Unda, the Bride of the Sea.

EPILOGUE

As the rash fool, a prey of Unda's art,
Drown thro' the passion of his fever'd heart,
So are our youth, inflam'd by tempters fair,
Bereft of reason and the manly air.
How sad the sight of Strephon's virile grace
Turn'd to confusion at his Chloë's face,
And e'er Pelides, dear to Grecian eyes,
Sulking for loss of his thrice-cherish'd prize.
Brothers, attend! If cares too sharply vex,
Gain rest by shunning the destructive sex!

FIRST PUBLISHED IN
The Providence Amateur, February 1916

LINES ON
GEN. ROBERT EDWARD LEE

Born Jan. 19, 1807

"*Si veris magna paratur*
Fama bonis, et si successu nuda remoto
Inspicitur virtus, quicquid laudamus in ullo
Majorum, fortuna fuit."
—Lucan

Whilst martial echoes o'er the wave resound,
And Europe's gore incarnadines the ground;
Today no foreign hero we bemoan,
But count the glowing virtues of our own!
Illustrious LEE! around whose honour'd name
Entwines a patriot's and a Christian's fame;
With whose just praise admiring nations ring,
And whom repenting foes contritely sing!
When first our land fraternal fury bore,
And Sumter's guns alarm'd the anxious shore;
When Faction's reign ancestral rights o'erthrew,
And sunder'd States a mutual hatred knew;
Then clash'd contending chiefs of kindred line,
In flesh to suffer and in fame to shine.
But o'er them all, majestic in his might,
Rose LEE, unrivall'd, to sublimest height:
With torturing choice defy'd opposing Fate,
And shunn'd Temptation for his native State!
Thus Washington his monarch's rule o'erturn'd

30

When young Columbia with rebellion burn'd.
And what in Washington the world reveres,
In LEE with equal magnitude appears.
Our nation's Father, crown'd with vict'ry's bays,
Enjoys a loving land's eternal praise:
Let, then, our hearts with equal rev'rence greet
His proud successor, rising o'er defeat!
Around his greatness pour disheartening woes,
But still he tow'rs above his conqu'ring foes.
Silence! ye jackal herd that vainly blame
Th' unspotted leader by a traitor's name:
If such was LEE, let blushing Justice mourn,
And trait'rous Liberty endure our scorn!
As Philopoemen once sublimely strove,
And earn'd declining Hellas' thankful love;
So follow'd LEE the purest patriot's part,
And wak'd the worship of the grateful heart:
The South her soul in body'd form discerns;
The North from LEE a nobler freedom learns!
Attend! ye sons of Albion's ancient race,
Whate'er your country, and whate'er your place:
LEE'S valiant deeds, tho' dear to Southern song,
To all our Saxon strain as well belong.
Courage like his the parent Island won,
And led an Empire past the setting sun;
To realms unknown our laws and language bore;
Rais'd England's banner on the desert shore;
Crush'd the proud rival, and subdu'd the sea
For ages past, and aeons yet to be!
From Scotia's hilly bounds the paean rolls,
And Afric's distant Cape great LEE extols;
The sainted soul and manly mien combine
To grace Britannia's and Virginia's line!
As dullards now in thoughtless fervour prate
Of shameful peace, and sing th' unmanly State;

As churls their piping reprobations shriek,
And damn the heroes that protect the weak;
Let LEE'S brave shade the timid throng accost,
And give them back the manhood they have lost!
What kindlier spirit, breathing from on high,
Can teach us how to live and how to die?

FIRST PUBLISHED IN
The Coyote, January 1917

TO PAN

Seated in a woodland glen
By a shallow reedy stream
Once I fell a-musing, when
I was lull'd into a dream.

From the brook a shape arose
Half a man and half a goat.
Hoofs it had instead of toes
And a beard adorn'd its throat

On a set of rustic reeds
Sweetly play'd this hybrid man
Naught car'd I for earthly needs,
For I knew that this was *Pan*

Nymphs & Satyrs gather'd 'round
To enjoy the lively sound.

All to soon I woke in pain
And return'd to haunts of men.
But in rural vales I'd fain
Live and hear *Pan's* pipes again.

FIRST PUBLISHED IN
The Tryout, April 1919

AN
AMERICAN TO
MOTHER ENGLAND

England! My England! Can the surging sea
That lies between us tear my heart from thee?
Can distant birth and distant dwelling drain
Th' ancestral blood that warms the loyal vein?
Isle of my Fathers! hear the filial song
Of him whose sources but to thee belong!
World-conquering Mother! by thy mighty hand
Was carv'd from savage wilds my native land:
Thy matchless sons the firm foundation laid;
Thy matchless arts the nascent nation made:
By thy just laws the young republic grew,
And thro' thy greatness, kindred greatness knew:
What man that springs from thy untainted line
But sees Columbia's virtues all as thine?
Whilst nameless multitudes upon our shore
From the dim corners of creation pour,
Whilst mongrel slaves crawl hither to partake
Of Saxon liberty they could not make,
From such an alien crew in grief I turn,
And for the mother's voice of Britain burn.
England! Can aught remove the cherish'd chain
That binds my spirit to thy blest domain?
Can Revolution's bitter precepts sway
The soul that must the ties of race obey?

Create a new Columbia if ye will;
The flesh that forms me is Britannic still!
Hail! oaken shades, and meads of dewy green,
So oft in sleep, yet ne'er in waking seen.
Peal out, ye ancient chimes, from vine-clad tow'r
Where pray'd my fathers in a vanish'd hour:
What countless years of rev'rence can ye claim
From bygone worshippers that bore my name!
Their forms are crumbling in the vaults around,
Whilst I, across the sea, but dream the sound.
Return, Sweet Vision! Let me glimpse again
The stone-built abbey, rising o'er the plain;
The neighb'ring village with its sun-show'r'd square;
The shaded mill-stream, and the forest fair,
The hedge-lin'd lane, that leads to rustic cot
Where sweet contentment is the peasant's lot;
The mystic grove, by Druid wraiths possess'd,
The flow'ring fields, with fairy-castles blest:
And the old manor-house, sedate and dark,
Set in the shadows of the wooded park.
Can this be dreaming? Must my eyelids close
That I may catch the fragrance of the rose?
Is it in fancy that the midnight vale
Thrills with the warblings of the nightingale?
A golden moon bewitching radiance yields,
And England's fairies trip o'er England's fields.
England! Old England! in my love for thee
No dream is mine, but blessed memory;
Such haunting images and hidden fires
Course with the bounding blood of British sires:
From British bodies, minds, and souls I come,
And from them draw the vision of their home.
Awake, Columbia! scorn the vulgar age

That bids thee slight thy lordly heritage.
Let not the wide Atlantic's wildest wave
Burst the blest bonds that fav'ring Nature gave:
Connecting surges 'twixt the nations run,
Our Saxon souls dissolving into one!

FIRST PUBLISHED IN
Poesy, January 1916

THE ROSE
OF ENGLAND

At morn the rosebud greets the sun
  And sheds the evening dew,
Expanding ere the day is done,
  In bloom of radiant hue;
And when the sun his rest hath found,
Rose-petals strow the garden round!

Thus that blest Isle that owns the Rose
  From mist and darkness came,
A million glories to disclose,
  And spread BRITANNIA's name;
And ere Life's Sun shall leave the blue,
ENGLAND shall reign the whole world thro'!

FIRST PUBLISHED IN
The Scot, October 1916

THE POE-ET'S
NIGHTMARE

A FABLE

Luxus tumultus semper causa est.

Lucullus Languish, student of the skies,
And connoisseur of rarebits and mince pies,
A bard by choice, a grocer's clerk by trade,
(Grown pessimist thro' honours long delay'd),
A secret yearning bore, that he might shine
In breathing numbers, and in song divine.
Each day his fountain pen was wont to drop
An ode or dirge or two about the shop,
Yet naught could strike the chord within his heart
That throbb'd for poesy, and cry'd for art.
Each eve he sought his bashful Muse to wake
With overdoses of ice-cream and cake;
But thou' th' ambitious youth a dreamer grew,
Th' Aonian Nymph declin'd to come to view.
Sometimes at dusk he scour'd the heav'ns afar,
Searching for raptures in the evening star;
One night he strove to catch a tale untold
In crystal deeps—but only caught a cold.
So pin'd Lucullus with his lofty woe,
Till one drear day he bought a set of Poe:
Charm'd with the cheerful horrors there display'd,
He vow'd with gloom to woo the Heav'nly Maid.
Of Auber's tarn and Yaanek's slope he dreams,

And weaves an hundred Ravens in his schemes.
Not far from our young hero's peaceful home
Lies the fair grove wherein he loves to roam.
Tho' but a stunted copse in vacant lot,
He dubs it Tempe, and adores the spot;
When shallow puddles dot the wooded plain,
And brim o'er muddy banks with muddy rain,
He calls them limpid lakes or poison pools
(Depending on which bard his fancy rules).
'Tis here he comes with Heliconian fire
On Sundays when he smites the Attic lyre;
And here one afternoon he brought his gloom,
Resolv'd to chant a poet's lay of doom.
Roget's Thesaurus, and a book of rhymes,
Provide the rungs whereon his spirit climbs:
With this grave retinue he trod the grove
And pray'd the Fauns he might a Poe-et prove.
But sad to tell, ere Pegasus flew high,
The not unrelish'd supper hour drew nigh;
Our tuneful swain th' imperious call attends,
And soon above the groaning table bends.
Tho' it were too prosaic to relate
Th' exact particulars of what he ate
(Such long-drawn lists the hasty reader skips,
Like Homer's well-known catalogue of ships),
This much we swear: that as adjournment near'd,
A monstrous lot of cake had disappear'd!
Soon to his chamber the young bard repairs,
And courts soft Somnus with sweet Lydian airs;
Thro' open casement scans the star-strown deep,
And 'neath Orion's beams sinks off to sleep.
Now start from airy dell the elfin train
That dance each midnight o'er the sleeping plain,
To bless the just, or cast a warning spell
On those who dine not wisely, but too well.

First Deacon Smith they plague, whose nasal glow
Comes from what Holmes hath call'd "Elixir Pro";
Group'd round the couch his visage they deride,
Whilst thro' his dreams unnumber'd serpents glide.
Next troop the little folk into the room
Where snores our young Endymion, swath'd in gloom:
A smile lights up his boyish face, whilst he
Dreams of the moon—or what he ate at tea.
The chieftain elf th' unconscious youth surveys,
And on his form a strange enchantment lays:
Those lips, that lately thrill'd with frosted cake,
Uneasy sounds in slumbrous fashion make;
At length their owner's fancies they rehearse,
And lisp this awesome Poe-em in blank verse:

ALETHEIA PHRIKODES

Omnia risus et omnia pulvis et omnia nihil.

Demoniac clouds, up-pil'd in chasmy reach
Of soundless heav'n, smother'd the brooding night;
Nor came the wonted whisp'rings of the swamp,
Nor voice of autumn wind along the moor,
Nor mutter'd noises of th' insomnious grove
Whose black recesses never saw the sun.
Within that grove a hideous hollow lies,
Half bare of trees; a pool in centre lurks
That none dares sound; a tarn of murky face
(Tho' naught can prove its hue, since light of day,
Affrighted, shuns the forest-shadow'd banks).
Hard by, a yawning hillside grotto breathes,
From deeps unvisited, a dull, dank air
That sears the leaves on certain stunted trees
Which stand about, clawing the spectral gloom

40

With evil boughs. To this accursed dell
Come woodland creatures, seldom to depart:
Once I behold, upon a crumbling stone
Set altar-like before the cave, a thing
I saw not clearly, yet from glimpsing, fled.
In this half-dusk I meditate alone
At many a weary noontide, when without
A world forgets me in its sun-blest mirth.
Here howl by night the werewolves, and the souls
Of those that knew me well in other days.
Yet on this night the grove spake not to me;
Nor spake the swamp, nor wind along the moor,
Nor moan'd the wind about the lonely eaves
Of the bleak, haunted pile wherein I lay.
I was afraid to sleep, or quench the spark
Of the low-burning taper by my couch.
I was afraid when thro' the vaulted space
Of the old tow'r, the clock-ticks died away
Into a silence so profound and chill
That my teeth chatter'd—giving yet no sound.
Then flicker'd low the light, and all dissolv'd,
Leaving me floating in the hellish grasp
Of body'd blackness, from whose beating wings
Came ghoulish blasts of charnel-scented mist.
Things vague, unseen, unfashion'd, and unnam'd
Jostled each other in the seething void
That gap'd, chaotic, downward to a sea
Of speechless horror, foul with writhing thoughts.
All this I felt, and felt the mocking eyes
Of the curs'd universe upon my soul;
Yet naught I saw nor heard, till flash'd a beam
Of lurid lustre thro' the rotting heav'ns,
Playing on scenes I labour'd not to see.
Methought the nameless tarn, alight at last,
Reflected shapes, and more reveal'd within

41

Those shocking depths than ne'er were seen before;
Methought from out the cave a demon train,
Grinning and smirking, reel'd in fiendish rout;
Bearing within their reeking paws a load
Of carrion viands for an impious feast.
Methought the stunted trees with hungry arms
Grop'd greedily for things I dare not name;
The while a stifling, wraith-like noisomeness
Fill'd all the dale, and spoke a larger life
Of uncorporeal hideousness awake
In the half-sentient wholeness of the spot.
Now glow'd the ground, and tarn, and cave, and trees,
And moving forms, and things not spoken of,
With such a phosphorescence as men glimpse
In the putrescent thickets of the swamp
Where logs decaying lie, and rankness reigns.
Methought a fire-mist drap'd with lucent fold
The well-remember'd features of the grove,
Whilst whirling ether bore in eddying streams
The hot, unfinish'd stuff of nascent worlds
Hither and thither thro' infinities
Of light and darkness, strangely intermix'd;
Wherein all entity had consciousness,
Without th' accustom'd outward shape of life.
Of these swift-circling currents was my soul,
Free from the flesh, a true constituent part;
Nor felt I less myself, for want of form.
Then clear'd the mist, and o'er a star-strown scene,
Divine and measureless, I gaz'd in awe.
Alone in space, I view'd a feeble fleck
Of silvern light, marking the narrow ken
Which mortals call the boundless universe.
On ev'ry side, each as a tiny star,
Shone more creations, vaster than our own,
And teeming with unnumber'd forms of life;

Tho' we as life would recognise it not,
Being bound to earthy thoughts of human mould.
As on a moonless night the Milky Way
In solid sheen displays its countless orbs
To weak terrestrial eyes, each orb a sun;
So beam'd the prospect on my wond'ring soul:
A spangled curtain, rich with twinkling gems,
Yet each a mighty universe of suns.
But as I gaz'd, I sens'd a spirit voice
In speech didactic, tho' no voice it was,
Save as it carried thought. It bade me mark
That all the universes in my view
Form'd but an atom in infinity;
Whose reaches pass the ether-laden realms
Of heat and light, extending to far fields
Where flourish worlds invisible and vague,
Fill'd with strange wisdom and uncanny life,
And yet beyond; to myriad spheres of light,
To spheres of darkness, to abysmal voids
That know the pulses of disorder'd force.
Big with these musings, I survey'd the surge
Of boundless being, yet I us'd not eyes,
For spirit leans not on the props of sense.
The docent presence swell'd my strength of soul;
All things I knew, but knew with mind alone.
Time's endless vista spread before my thought
With its vast pageant of unceasing change
And sempiternal strife of force and will;
I saw the ages flow in stately stream
Past rise and fall of universe and life;
I saw the birth of suns and worlds, their death,
Their transmutation into limpid flame,
Their second birth and second death, their course
Perpetual thro' the aeons' termless flight,
Never the same, yet born again to serve

The varying purpose of omnipotence.
And whilst I watch'd, I knew each second's space
Was greater than the lifetime of our world.
Then turn'd my musings to that speck of dust
Whereon my form corporeal took its rise;
That speck, born but a second, which must die
In one brief second more; that fragile earth;
That crude experiment; that cosmic sport
Which holds our proud, aspiring race of mites
And moral vermin; those presuming mites
Whom ignorance with empty pomp adorns,
And misinstructs in specious dignity;
Those mites who, reas'ning outward, vaunt themselves
As the chief work of Nature, and enjoy
In fatuous fancy the particular care
Of all her mystic, super-regnant pow'r.
And as I strove to vision the sad sphere
Which lurk'd, lost in ethereal vortices,
Methough my soul, tun'd to the infinite,
Refus'd to glimpse that poor atomic blight;
That misbegotten accident of space;
That globe of insignificance, whereon
(My guide celestial told me) dwells no part
Of empyrean virtue, but where breed
The coarse corruptions of divine disease;
The fest'ring ailments of infinity;
The morbid matter by itself call'd man:
Such matter (said my guide) as oft breaks forth
On broad Creation's fabric, to annoy
For a brief instant, ere assuaging death
Heal up the malady its birth provok'd.
Sicken'd, I turn'd my heavy thoughts away.
Then spake th' ethereal guide with mocking mien,
Upbraiding me for searching after Truth;
Visiting on my mind the searing scorn

Of mind superior; laughing at the woe
Which rent the vital essence of my soul.
Methought he brought remembrance of the time
When from my fellows to the grove I stray'd,
In solitude and dusk to meditate
On things forbidden, and to pierce the veil
Of seeming good and seeming beauteousness
That covers o'er the tragedy of Truth,
Helping mankind forget his sorry lot,
And raising Hope where Truth would crush it down.
He spake, and as he ceas'd, methought the flames
Of fuming Heav'n resolv'd in torments dire;
Whirling in maelstroms of rebellious might,
Yet ever bound by laws I fathom'd not.
Cycles and epicycles, of such girth
That each a cosmos seem'd, dazzled my gaze
Till all a wild phantasmal glow became.
Now burst athwart the fulgent formlessness
A rift of purer sheen, a sight supernal,
Broader that all the void conceiv'd by man,
Yet narrow here. A glimpse of heav'ns beyond;
Of weird creations so remote and great
That ev'n my guide assum'd a tone of awe.
Borne on the wings of stark immensity,
A touch of rhythm celestial reach'd my soul;
Thrilling me more with horror than with joy.
Again the spirit mock'd my human pangs,
And deep revil'd me for presumptuous thoughts:
Yet changing now his mien, he bade me scan
The wid'ning rift that clave the walls of space;
He bade me search it for the ultimate;
He bade me find the Truth I sought so long;
He bade me brave th' unutterable Thing,
The final Truth of moving entity.
All this he bade and offer'd—but my soul,

Clinging to life, fled without aim or knowledge,
Shrieking in silence thro' the gibbering deeps.

Thus shriek'd the young Lucullus, as he fled
Thro' gibbering deeps—and tumbled out of bed;
Within the room the morning sunshine gleams,
Whilst the poor youth recalls his troubled dreams.
He feels his aching limbs, whose woeful pain
Informs his soul his body lives again,
And thanks his stars—or cosmoses—or such
That he survives the noxious nightmare's clutch.
Thrill'd with the music of th' eternal spheres
(Or is it the alarm-clock that he hears?),
He vows to all the Pantheon, high and low,
No more to feed on cake, or pie, or Poe.
And now his gloomy spirits seem to rise,
As he the world beholds with clearer eyes;
The cup he thought too full of dregs to quaff
Affords him wine enough to raise a laugh.
(All this is metaphor—you must not think
Our late Endymion prone to stronger drink!)
With brighter visage and with lighter heart,
He turns his fancies to the grocer's mart;
And strange to say, at last he seems to find
His daily duties worthy of his mind.
Since Truth prov'd such a high and dang'rous goal,
Our bard seeks one less trying to his soul;
With deep-drawn breath he flouts his dreary woes,
And a good clerk from a bad poet grows!
Now close attend my lay, ye scribbling crew
That bay the moon in numbers strange and new;
That madly for the spark celestial bawl
In metres short or long, or none at all:
Curb your rash force, in numbers or at tea,
Nor overzealous for high fancies be;

Reflect, ere ye the draught Pierian take,
What worthy clerks or plumbers ye might make;
Wax not too frenzied in the leaping line
That neither sense nor measure can confine,
Lest ye, like young Lucullus Launguish, groan
Beneath Poe-etic nightmares of your own!

First published in
The Vagrant, July 1918

FACT AND FANCY

———————————

How dull the wretch, whose philosophic mind
Disdains the pleasures of fantastic kind;
Whose prosy thoughts the joys of life exclude,
And wreck the solace of the poet's mood!
Young Zeno, practic'd in the Stoic's art,
Rejects the language of the glowing heart;
Dissolves sweet Nature to a mess of laws;
Condemns th' effect whilst looking for the cause;
Freezes poor Ovid in an ic'd review,
And sneers because his fables are untrue!
In search of Truth the hopeful zealot goes,
But all the sadder tums, the more he knows!
Stay! vandal sophist, whose deep lore would blast
The graceful legends of the story'd past;
Whose tongue in censure flays th' embellish'd page,
And scolds the comforts of a dreary age:
Would'st strip the foliage from the vital bough
Till all men grow as wisely dull as thou?
Happy the man whose fresh, untainted eye
Discerns a Pantheon in the spangled sky;
Finds Sylphs and Dryads in the waving trees,
And spies soft Notus in the southern breeze;
For whom the stream a cheering carol sings,
While reedy music by the fountain rings;
To whom the waves a Nereid tale confide
Till friendly presence fills the rising tide.
Happy is he, who void of learning's woes,

Th' ethereal life of body'd Nature knows:
I scorn the sage that tells me it but seems,
And flout his gravity in sunlit dreams!

FIRST PUBLISHED IN
The Tryout, February 1917

PACIFIST WAR SONG

1917

We are the valiant Knights of Peace
   Who prattle for the Right:
Our banner is of snowy fleece,
   Inscribed: "Too Proud To Fight!"

By sweet Chautauqua's flow'ry banks
   We love to sing and play,
But should we spy a foeman's ranks,
   We'd proudly run away!

When Prussian fury sweeps the main
   Our freedom to deny;
Of tyrant laws we ne'er complain,
   But gladsomely comply!

We do not fear the submarines
   That plough the troubled foam;
We scorn the ugly old machines—
   And safely stay at home!

They say our country's close to war,
   And soon must man the guns;
But we see naught to struggle for—
   We love the gentle Huns!

What tho' their hireling Greaser bands
   Invade our southern plains?
We well can spare those boist'rous lands,
   Content with what remains!

Our fathers were both rude and bold,
   And would not live like brothers;
But we are of a finer mould—
   We're much more like our mothers!

FIRST PUBLISHED IN
The Tryout, March 1917

A GARDEN

There's an ancient, ancient garden that I see sometimes in dreams,
Where the very Maytime sunlight plays and glows with spectral gleams;
Where the gaudy-tinted blossoms seem to wither into grey,
And the crumbling walls and pillars waken thoughts of yesterday.
There are vines in nooks and crannies, and there's moss about the pool,
And the tangled weedy thicket chokes the arbour dark and cool:
In the silent sunken pathways springs an herbage sparse and spare,
Where the musty scent of dead things dulls the fragrance of the air.
There is not a living creature in the lonely space around,
And the hedge-encompass'd quiet never echoes to a sound.
As I walk, and wait, and listen, I will often seek to find
When it was I knew that garden in an age long left behind;
I will oft conjure a vision of a day that is no more,
As I gaze upon the grey, grey scenes I feel I knew before.
Then a sadness settles o'er me, and a tremor seems to start:
For I know the flow'rs are shrivell'd hopes—the garden is my heart!

FIRST PUBLISHED IN
The Vagrant, Spring 192

THE
PEACE ADVOCATE

_____

Supposed to be a "pome,"
but cast strictly in modern metre.

The vicar sat in the firelight's glow,
    A volume in his hand;
  And a tear he shed for the widespread woe,
  And the anguish brought by the vicious foe
    That overran the land.

But ne'er a hand for his King rais'd he,
    For he was a man of peace;
  And he car'd not a whit for the victory
  That must come to preserve his nation free,
    And the world from fear release.

His son had buckled on his sword,
    The first at the front was he;
  But the vicar his valiant child ignor'd,
  And his noble deeds in the field deplor'd,
    For he knew not bravery.

On his flock he strove to fix his will,
    And lead them to scorn the fray.
  He told them that conquest brings but ill;
  That meek submission would serve them still
    To keep the foe away.

In vain did he hear the bugle's sound
     That strove to avert the fall.
  The land, quoth he, is all men's ground,
  What matter if friend or foe be found
     As master of us all?

One day from the village green hard by
     The vicar heard a roar
  Of cannon that rivall'd the anguish'd cry
  Of the hundreds that liv'd, but wish'd to die
     As the enemy rode them o'er.

Now he sees his own cathedral shake
     At the foeman's wanton aim.
  The ancient tow'rs with the bullets quake;
  The steeples fall, the foundations break,
     And the whole is lost in flame.

Up the vicarage lane file the cavalcade,
     And the vicar, and daughter, and wife
  Scream out in vain for the needed aid
  That only a regiment might have made
     Ere they lose what is more than life.

Then quick to his brain came manhood's thought,
     As he saw his erring course;
  And the vicar his dusty rifle brought
  That the foe might at least by one be fought,
     And force repaid with force.

One shot—the enemy's blasting fire
     A breach in the wall cuts thro',
  But the vicar replies with his waken'd ire;
  Fells one arm'd brute for each fallen spire,

And in blood is born anew.

Two shots—the wife and daughter sink,
      Each with a mortal wound;
   And the vicar, too madden'd by far to think,
   Rushes boldly on to death's vague brink,
      With the manhood he has found.

Three shots—but shots of another kind
      The smoky regions rend;
   And upon the foeman with rage gone blind,
   Like a ceaseless, resistless, avenging wind,
      The rescuing troops descend.

The smoke-pall clears, and the vicar's son
      His father's life has sav'd;
   And the vicar looks o'er the ruin done,
   Ere the vict'ry by his child was won,
      His face with care engrav'd.

The vicar sat in the firelight's glow,
      The volume in his hand,
   That brought to his hearth the bitter woe
   Which only a husband and father can know,
      And truly understand.

With a chasten'd mien he flung the book
      To the leaping flames before;
   And a breath of sad relief he took
   As the pages blacken'd beneath his look—
      The fool of Peace no more!

EPILOGUE

The rev'rend parson, wak'd to man's estate,
Laments his wife's and daughter's common fate.
His martial son in warm embrace enfolds,
And clings the tighter to the child he holds.
His peaceful notions, banish'd in an hour,
Will nevermore his wit or sense devour;
But steep'd in truth, 'tis now his nobler plan
To cure, yet recognise, the faults of man.

FIRST PUBLISHED IN
The Tryout, May 1917

ODE FOR
JULY FOURTH, 1917

As Columbia's brave scions, in anger array'd,
  Once defy'd a proud monarch and built a new nation;
'Gainst their brothers of Britain
unsheath'd the sharp blade
  That hath ne'er met defeat nor endur'd desecration;
     So must we in this hour
     Show our valour and pow'r,
And dispel the black perils that over us low'r:
  Whilst the sons of Britannia, no longer our foes,
  Will rejoice in our triumphs and strengthen our blows!

See the banners of Liberty float in the breeze
  That plays light o'er the regions our fathers defended;
Hear the voice of the million resound o'er the leas,
  As the deeds of the past are proclaim'd and commended;
     And in splendour on high
     Where our flags proudly fly,
See the folds we tore down flung again to the sky:
  For the Emblem of England, in kinship unfurl'd,
  Shall divide with Old Glory the praise of the world!

Bury'd now are the hatreds of subject and King,
   And the strife that once sunder'd
an Empire hath vanish'd.
With the fame of the Saxon the heavens shall ring
   As the vultures of darkness are baffled and banish'd;
      And the broad British sea,
      Of her enemies free,
Shall in tribute bow gladly, Columbia to thee:
   For the friends of the Right, in the field side by side,
   Form a fabric of Freedom no hand can divide!

FIRST PUBLISHED IN
The United Amateur, July 1917

NEMESIS

Thro' the ghoul-guarded gateways of slumber,
  Past the wan-moon'd abysses of night,
 I have liv'd o'er my lives without number,
  I have sounded all things with my sight;
And I struggle and shriek ere the daybreak, being driven to madness
  with fright.

  I have whirl'd with the earth at the dawning,
   When the sky was a vaporous flame;
  I have seen the dark universe yawning,
   Where the black planets roll without aim;
Where they roll in their horror unheeded, without knowledge or
  lustre or name.

  I had drifted o'er seas without ending,
   Under sinister grey-clouded skies
  That the many-fork'd lightning is rending,
   That resound with hysterical cries;
With the moans of invisible daemons that out of the green waters
  rise.

  I have plung'd like a deer thro' the arches
   Of the hoary primordial grove,
  Where the oaks feel the presence that marches
   And stalks on where no spirit dares rove;
And I flee from a thing that surrounds me, and leers thro' dead
  branches above.

I have stumbled by cave-ridden mountains
    That rise barren and bleak from the plain,
I have drunk of the fog-foetid fountains
    That ooze down to the marsh and the main;
And in hot cursed tarns I have seen things I care not to gaze on again.

I have scann'd the vast ivy-clad palace,
    I have trod its untenanted hall,
Where the moon writhing up from the valleys
    Shews the tapestried things on the wall;
Strange figures discordantly woven, which I cannot endure to recall.

I have peer'd from the casement in wonder
    At the mouldering meadows around,
At the many-roof'd village laid under
    The curse of a grave-girdled ground;
And from rows of white urn-carven marble I listen intently for sound.

I have haunted the tombs of the ages,
    I have flown on the pinions of fear
Where the smoke-belching Erebus rages,
    Where the jokulls loom snow-clad and drear:
And in realms where the sun of the desert consumes what it never can
    cheer.

I was old when the Pharaohs first mounted
    The jewel-deck'd throne by the Nile;
I was old in those epochs uncounted
    When I, and I only, was vile;
And Man, yet untainted and happy, dwelt in bliss on the far Arctic isle.

Oh, great was the sin of my spirit,
 And great is the reach of its doom;
Not the pity of Heaven can cheer it,
 Nor can respite be found in the tomb:
Down the infinite aeons come beating the wings of unmerciful gloom.

Thro' the ghoul-guarded gateways of slumber,
 Past the wan-moon'd abysses of night,
I have liv'd o'er my lives without number,
 I have sounded all things with my sight;
And I struggle and shriek ere the daybreak, being driven to madness with
 fright.

First published in
The Vagrant, June 1918

ASTROPHOBOS

In the midnight heavens burning
   Thro' ethereal deeps afar,
Once I watch'd with restless yearning
   An alluring, aureate star;
Ev'ry eye aloft returning,
   Gleaming nigh the Arctic car.

Mystic waves of beauty blended
   With the gorgeous golden rays;
Phantasies of bliss descended
   In a myrrh'd Elysian haze;
And in lyre-born chords extended
   Harmonies of Lydian lays.

There (thought I) lies scenes of pleasure,
   Where the free and blessed dwell,
And each moment bears a treasure
   Freighted with a lotus-spell,
And there floats a liquid measure
   From the lute of Israfel.

There (I told myself) were shining
   Worlds of happiness unknown,
Peace and Innocence entwining
   By the Crowned Virtue's throne;
Men of light, their thoughts refining
   Purer, fairer, than our own.

Thus I mus'd, when o'er the vision
  Crept a red delirious change;
Hope dissolving to derision,
  Beauty to distortion strange;
Hymnic chords in weird collision,
  Spectral sights in endless range.

Crimson burn'd the star of sadness
  As behind the beams I peer'd;
All was woe that seem'd but gladness
  Ere my gaze with truth was sear'd;
Cacodaemons, mir'd with madness,
  Thro' the fever'd flick'ring leer'd.

Now I know the fiendish fable
  That the golden glitter bore;
Now I shun the spangled sable
  That I watch'd and lov'd before;
But the horror, set and stable,
  Haunts my soul for evermore.

First published in
The United Amateur, January 1918

SUNSET

The cloudless day is richer at its close;
  A golden glory settles on the lea;
Soft, stealing shadows hint of cool repose
  To mellowing landscape, and to calming sea.

And in that nobler, gentler, lovelier light,
  The soul to sweeter, loftier bliss inclines;
Freed form the noonday glare, the favour'd sight
  Increasing grace in earth and sky divines.

But ere the purest radiance crowns the green,
  Or fairest lustre fills th' expectant grove,
The twilight thickens, and the fleeting scene
  Leaves but a hallow'd memory of love!

FIRST PUBLISHED IN
The Tryout, December 1917

LAETA

A LAMENT

Respectfully Dedicated to
RHEINHART KLEINER, Esq.
With Compliments of the Author

How sad droop the willows by Zulal's fair side,
Where so lately I stray'd with my raven-hair'd bride:
Ev'ry light-floating lily, each flow'r on the shore,
Folds in sorrow since Laeta can see them no more!

Oh, blest were the days when in childhood and hope
With my Laeta I rov'd o'er the blossom-clad slope,
Plucking white meadow-daisies and ferns by the stream,
As we laugh'd at the ripples that twinkle and gleam.

Not a bloom deck'd the mead that could rival in grace
The dear innocent charms of my Laeta's fair face;
Not a thrush thrill'd the grove with a carol so choice
As the silvery strains of my Laeta's sweet voice.

The shy Nymphs of the woodland, the fount and the plain,
Strove to equal her beauty, but strove all in vain;
Yet no envy they bore her, while fruitless they strove,
For so pure was my Laeta, they could only love!

When the warm breath of Auster play'd soft o'er the flow'rs,
And young Zephyrus rustled the gay scented bow'rs,
Ev'ry breeze seem'd to pause as it drew near the fair,
Too much aw'd at her sweetness to tumble her hair.

How fond were our dreams on the day when we stood
In the ivy-grown temple beside the dark wood;
When our pledges we seal'd at the sanctify'd shrine,
And I knew that my Laeta forever was mine!

How blissful our thoughts when the wild autumn came,
And the forests with scarlet and gold were aflame;
Yet how heavy my heart when I first felt the fear
That my starry-eyed Laeta would fade with the year!

The pastures were sere and the heavens were grey
When I laid my lov'd Laeta forever away,
And the river god pity'd, as weeping I pac'd
Mingling hot bitter tears with his cold frozen waste.

Now the flow'rs have return'd, but they bloom not so sweet
As in days when they blossom'd round Laeta's dear feet;
And the willows complain to the answering hill,
And the thrushes that once were so happy are still.

The green meadows and groves in their loneliness pine,
Whilst the Dryads no more in their madrigals join,
The breeze once so joyous now murmurs and sighs,
And blows soft o'er the spot where my lov'd Laeta lies.

So pensive I roam o'er the desolate lawn
Where we wander'd and lov'd in the days that are gone,
And I yearn for the autumn, when Zulal's blue tide
Shall sing low by my grave at the lov'd Laeta's side.

FIRST PUBLISHED IN
The Tryout, February 1918

PSYCHOPOMPOS

_____

A TALE IN RHYME

I am He who howls in the night;
   I am He who moans in the snow;
I am He who hath never seen light;
   I am He who mounts from below.

My car is the car of Death;
   My wings are the wings of dread;
My breath is the north wind's breath;
   My prey are the cold and the dead.

In old Auvergne, when schools were poor and few,
And peasants fancy'd what they scarcely knew,
When lords and gentry shunn'd their Monarch's throne
For solitary castles of their own,
There dwelt a man of rank, whose fortress stood
In the hush'd twilight of a hoary wood.
De Blois his name; his lineage high and vast,
A proud memorial of an honour'd past;
But curious swains would whisper now and then
That Sieur De Blois was not as other men.
In person dark and lean, with glossy hair,
And gleaming teeth that he would often bare,
With piercing eye, and stealthy roving glance,
And tongue that clipt the soft, sweet speech of France;
The Sieur was little lov'd and seldom seen,
So close he kept within his own demesne.

The castle servants, few, discreet, and old,
Full many a tale of strangeness might have told;
But bow'd with years, they rarely left the door
Wherein their sires and grandsires serv'd before.
Thus gossip rose, as gossip rises best,
When mystery imparts a keener zest;
Seclusion oft the poison tongue attracts,
And scandal prospers on a dearth of facts.
'Twas said, the Sieur had more than once been spy'd
Alone at midnight by the river's side,
With aspect so uncouth, and gaze so strange,
That rustics cross'd themselves to see the change;
Yet none, when press'd, could clearly say or know
Just what it was, or why they trembled so.
De Blois, as rumour whisper'd, fear'd to pray,
Nor us'd his chapel on the Sabbath day;
Howe'er this may have been, 'twas known at least
His household had no chaplain, monk, or priest.
But if the Master liv'd in dubious fame,
Twice fear'd and hated was his noble Dame;
As dark as he, in features wild and proud,
And with a weird supernal grace endow'd,
The haughty mistress scorn'd the rural train
Who sought to learn her source, but sought in vain.
Old women call'd her eyes too bright by half,
And nervous children shiver'd at her laugh;
Richard, the dwarf (whose word had little weight),
Vow'd she was like a serpent in her gait,
Whilst ancient Pierre (the aged often err)
Laid all her husband's mystery to her.
Still more absurd were those odd mutter'd things
That calumny to curious list'ners brings;
Those subtle slanders, told with downcast face,
And muffled voice—those tales no man may trace;
Tales that the faith of old wives can command,

69

Tho' always heard at sixth or seventh hand.
Thus village legend darkly would imply
That Dame De Blois possess'd an evil eye;
Or going further, furtively suggest
A lurking spark of sorcery in her breast;
Old Mère Allard (herself half witch) once said
The lady's glance work'd strangely on the dead.
So liv'd the pair, like many another two
That shun the crowd, and shrink from public view.
They scorn'd the doubts by ev'ry peasant shewn,
And ask'd but one thing—to be let alone!

'Twas Candlemas, the dreariest time of year,
With fall long gone, and spring too far to cheer,
When little Jean, the bailiff's son and heir,
Fell sick and threw the doctors in despair.
A child so stout and strong that few would think
An hour might carry him to death's dark brink,
Yet pale he lay, tho' hidden was the cause,
And Galens search'd in vain thro' Nature's laws.
But stricken sadness could not quite suppress
The roving thought, or wrinkled grandam's guess:
Tho' spoke by stealth, 'twas known to half a score
That Dame De Blois rode by the day before;
She had (they said) with glances weird and wild
Paus'd by the gate to view the prattling child,
Nor did they like the smile which seem'd to trace
New lines of evil on her proud, dark face.
These things they whisper'd, when the mother's cry
Told of the end—the gentle soul gone by;
In genuine grief the kindly watcher wept,
Whilst the lov'd babe with saints and angels slept.
The village priest his simple rites went thro',
And good Michel nail'd up the box of yew;
Around the corpse the holy candles burn'd,

The mourners sighed, the parents dumbly yearn'd.
Then one by one each sought his humble bed,
And left the lonely mother with her dead.
Late in the night it was, when o'er the vale
The storm-king swept with pandemoniac gale;
Deep pil'd the cruel snow, yet strange to tell,
The lightning sputter'd while the white flakes fell;
A hideous presence seem'd abroad to steal,
And terror sounded in the thunder's peal.
Within the house of grief the tapers glow'd
Whilst the poor mother bow'd beneath her load;
Her salty eyes too tired now to weep,
Too pain'd to see, too sad to close in sleep.
The clock struck three, above the tempest heard,
When something near the lifeless infant stirr'd;
Some slipp'ry thing, that flopp'd in awkward way,
And climb'd the table where the coffin lay;
With scaly convolutions strove to find
The cold, still clay that death had left behind.
The nodding mother hears—starts broad awake—
Empower'd to reason, yet too stunn'd to shake;
The pois'nous thing she sees, and nimbly foils
The ghoulish purpose of the quiv'ring coils:
With ready axe the serpent's head she cleaves,
And thrills with savage triumph whilst she grieves.
The injur'd reptile hissing glides from sight,
And hides its cloven carcass in the night.

The weeks slipp'd by, and gossip's tongue began
To call the Sieur De Blois an alter'd man;
With curious mien he oft would pace along
The village street, and eye the gaping throng.
Yet whilst he shew'd himself as ne'er before,
His wild-eyed lady was observ'd no more.
In course of time, 'twas scarce thought odd or ill

That he his ears with village lore should fill;
Nor was the town with special rumour rife
When he sought out the bailiff and his wife:
Their tale of sorrow, with its ghastly end,
Was told, indeed, by ev'ry wond'ring friend.
The Sieur heard all, and low'ring rode away,
Nor was he seen again for many a day.

When vernal sunshine shed its cheering glow,
And genial zephyrs blew away the snow,
To frighten'd swains a horror was reveal'd
In the damp herbage of a melting field.
There (half preserv'd by winter's frigid bed)
Lay the dark Dame De Blois, untimely dead;
By some assassin's stroke most foully slain,
Her shapely brow and temples cleft in twain.
Reluctant hands the dismal burden bore
To the stone arches of the husband's door,
Where silent serfs the ghastly thing receiv'd,
Trembling with fright, but less amaz'd than griev'd;
The Sieur his dame beheld with blazing eyes,
And shook with anger, more than with surprise.
(At least 'tis thus the stupid peasants told
Their wide-mouth'd wives when they the tale unroll'd.)
The village wonder'd why De Blois had kept
His spouse's loss unmention'd and unwept,
Nor were there lacking sland'rous tongues to claim
That the dark master was himself to blame.
But village talk could scarcely hope to solve
A crime so deep, and thus the months revolve:
The rural train repeat the gruesome tale,
And gape and marvel more than they bewail.

Swift flew the sun, and winter once again
With icy talons gripp'd the frigid plain.

December brought its store of Christmas cheer,
And grateful peasants hail'd the op'ning year;
But by the hearth as Candlemas drew nigh,
The whisp'ring ancients spoke of things gone by.
Few had forgot the dark demoniac lore
Of things that came the Candlemas before,
And many a crone intently eyed the house
Where dwelt the sadden'd bailiff and his spouse.
At last the day arriv'd, the sky o'erspread
With dark'ning messengers and clouds of lead;
Each neighb'ring grove Aeolian warnings sigh'd,
And thick'ning terrors broadcast seem'd to bide.
The good folk, tho' they knew not why, would run
Swift past the bailiff's door, the scene to shun;
Within the house the grieving couple wept,
And mourn'd the child who now forever slept.
On rush'd the dusk in doubly hideous form,
Borne on the pinions of the gath'ring storm;
Unusual murmurs fill'd the rainless wind,
The rising river lash'd the troubled shore;
Black thro' the night the awful storm-god prowl'd,
And froze the list'ners' life-blood as he howl'd;
Gigantic trees like supple rushes sway'd,
Whilst for his home the trembling cotter pray'd.
Now falls a sudden lull amidst the gale;
With less'ning force the circling currents wail;
Far down the stream that laves the neighb'ring mead
Burst a new ululation, wildly key'd;
The peasant train a frantic mien assume,
And huddle closer in the spectral gloom:
To each strain'd ear the truth too well is known,
For that dread sound can come from wolves alone!
The rustics close attend, when ere they think,
A lupine army swarms the river's brink;
From out the waters leap a howling train

73

That rend the air, and scatter o'er the plain:
With flaming orbs the frothing creatures fly,
And chant with hellish voice their hungry cry.
First of the pack a mighty monster leaps
With fearless tread, and martial order keeps;
Th' attendant wolves his yelping tones obey,
And form in columns for the coming fray:
No frighten'd swain they harm, but silent bound
With a fix'd purpose o'er the frozen ground.
Straight course the monsters thro' the village street,
Unholy vigour in their flying feet;
Thro' half-shut blinds the shelter'd peasants peer,
And wax in wonder as they lose in fear.
Th' excited pack at last their goal perceive,
And the vex'd air with deaf'ning clamour cleave;
The churls, astonish'd, watch th' unnatural herd
Flock round a cottage at the leader's word:
Quick spreads the fearsome fact, by rumour blown,
That the doom'd cottage is the bailiff's own!
Round and around the howling daemons glide,
Whilst the fierce leader scales the vine-clad side;
The frantic wind its horrid wail renews,
And mutters madly thro' the lifeless yews.
In the frail house the bailiff calmly waits
The rav'ning horde, and trusts th' impartial Fates,
But the wan wife revives with curious mien
Another monster and an older scene;
Amidst th' increasing wind that rocks the walls,
The dame to him the serpent's deed recalls:
Then as a nameless thought fills both their minds,
The bare-fang'd leader crashes thro' the blinds.
Across the room, with murd'rous fury rife,
Leaps the mad wolf, and seizes on the wife;
With strange intent he drags his shrieking prey
Close to the spot where once the coffin lay.

Wilder and wilder roars the mounting gale
That sweeps the hills and hurtles thro' the vale;
The ill-made cottage shakes, the pack without
Dance with new fury in demoniac rout.
Quick as his thought, the valiant bailiff stands
Above the wolf, a weapon in his hands;
The ready axe that serv'd a year before,
Now serves as well to slay one monster more.
The creature drops inert, with shatter'd head,
Full on the floor, and silent as the dead;
The rescu'd wife recalls the dire alarms,
And faints from terror in her husband's arms.
But as he holds her, all the cottage quakes,
And with full force the titan tempest breaks:
Down crash the walls, and o'er their shrinking forms
Burst the mad revels of the storm of storms.
Th' encircling wolves advance with ghastly pace,
Hunger and murder in each gleaming face,
But as they close, from out the hideous night
Flashes a bolt of unexpected light:
The vivid scene to ev'ry eye appears,
And peasants shiver with returning fears.
Above the wreck the scatheless chimney stays,
Its outline glimm'ring in the fitful rays,
Whilst o'er the hearth still hangs the household shrine,
The Saviour's image and the Cross divine!
Round the blest spot a lambent radiance glows,
And shields the cotters from their stealthy foes:
Each monstrous creature marks the wondrous glare,
Drops, fades, and vanishes in empty air!
The village train with startled eyes adore,
And count their beads in rev'rence o'er and o'er.
Now fades the light, and dies the raging blast,
The hour of dread and reign of horror past.
Pallid and bruis'd, from out his toppled walls

The panting bailiff with his good wife crawls:
Kind hands attend them, whilst o'er all the town
A strange sweet peace of spirit settles down.
Wonder and fear are still'd in soothing sleep,
As thro' the breaking clouds the moon rays peep.

Here paus'd the prattling grandam in her speech,
Confus'd with age, the tale half out of reach;
The list'ning guest, impatient for a clue,
Fears 'tis not one tale, but a blend of two;
He fain would know how far'd the widow'd lord
Whose eerie ways th' initial theme afford,
And marvels that the crone so quick should slight
His fate, to babble of the wolf-wrack'd night.
The old wife, press'd, for greater clearness strives,
Nods wisely, and her scatter'd wits revives;
Yet strangely lingers on her latter tale
Of wolf and bailiff, miracle and gale.
When (quoth the crone) the dawn's bright radiance bath'd
Th' eventful scene, so late in terror swath'd,
The chatt'ring churls that sought the ruin'd cot
Found a new marvel in the gruesome spot.
From fallen walls a trail of gory red,
As of the stricken wolf, erratic led;
O'er road and mead the new-dript crimson wound,
Till lost amidst the neighb'ring swampy ground:
With wonder unappeas'd the peasants burn'd,
For what the quicksand takes is ne'er return'd.

Once more the grandam, with a knowing eye,
Stops in her tale, to watch a hawk soar by;
The weary list'ner, baffled, seeks anew
For some plain statement, or enlight'ning clue.
Th' indulgent crone attends the puzzled plea,
Yet strangely mutters o'er the mystery.

The Sieur? Ah, yes—that morning all in vain
His shaking servants scour'd the frozen plain;
No man had seen him since he rode away
In silence on the dark preceding day.
His horse, wild-eyed with some unusual fright,
Came wand'ring from the river-bank that night.
His hunting-hound, that mourn'd with piteous woe,
Howl'd by the quicksand swamp, his grief to shew.
The village folk thought much, but utter'd less;
The servants' search wore out in emptiness:
For Sieur De Blois (the old wife's tale is o'er)
Was lost to mortal sight for evermore.

First published in
Vagrant, October 1919

DESPAIR

O'er the midnight moorlands crying,
Thro' the cypress forests sighing,
In the night-wind madly flying,
    Hellish forms with streaming hair;
In the barren branches creaking,
By the stagnant swamp-pools speaking,
Past the shore-cliffs ever shrieking;
    Damn'd daemons of despair.

Once, I think I half remember,
Ere the grey skies of November
Quench'd my youth's aspiring ember,
    Liv'd there such a thing as bliss;
Skies that now are dark were beaming,
Gold and azure, splendid seeming
Till I learn'd it all was dreaming—
    Deadly drowsiness of Dis.

But the stream of Time, swift flowing,
Brings the torment of half-knowing—
Dimly rushing, blindly going
    Past the never-trodden lea;
And the voyager, repining,
Sees the wicked death-fires shining,
Hears the wicked petrel's whining
    As he helpless drifts to sea.

Evil wings in ether beating;
Vultures at the spirit eating;
Things unseen forever fleeting
      Black against the leering sky.
Ghastly shades of bygone gladness,
Clawing fiends of future sadness,
Mingle in a cloud of madness
      Ever on the soul to lie.

Thus the living, lone and sobbing,
In the throes of anguish throbbing,
With the loathsome Furies robbing
      Night and noon of peace and rest.
But beyond the groans and grating
Of abhorrent Life, is waiting
Sweet Oblivion, culminating
      All the years of fruitless quest.

FIRST PUBLISHED IN
Pine Cones, June 1919

REVELATION

In a vale of light and laughter,
  Shining 'neath the friendly sun,
Where fulfilment follow'd after
  Ev'ry hope or dream begun;
Where an Aidenn gay and glorious,
  Beckon'd down the winsome way;
There my soul, o'er pain victorious,
  Laugh'd and lingered—yesterday.

Green and narrow was my valley,
  Temper'd with a verdant shade;
Sun-deck'd brooklets musically
  Sparkled thro' each glorious glade;
And at night the stars serenely
  Glow'd betwixt the boughs o'erhead,
While Astarte, calm and queenly,
  Floods of fairy radiance shed.

There amid the tinted bowers,
  Raptur'd with the opiate spell
Of the grasses, ferns, and flowers,
  Poppy, phlox and pimpernel,
Long I lay, entranc'd and dreaming,
  Pleas'd with Nature's bounteous store,
Till I mark'd the shaded gleaming
  Of the sky, and yearn'd for more.

Eagerly the branches tearing,
  Clear'd I all the space above,
Till the bolder gaze, high faring,
  Scann'd the naked skies of Jove;
Deeps unguess'd now shone before me,
  Splendid beam'd the solar car;
Wings of fervid fancy bore me
  Out beyond the farthest star.

Reaching, gasping, wishing, longing
  For the pageant brought to sight,
Vain I watch'd the gold orbs thronging
  Round celestial poles of light.
Madly on a moonbeam ladder
  Heav'n's abyss I sought to scale,
Ever wiser, ever sadder,
  As the fruitless task would fail.

Then, with futile striving sated,
  Veer'd my soul to earth again,
Well content that I was fated
  For a fair, yet low domain;
Pleasing thoughts of glad tomorrows,
  Like the blissful moments past,
Lull'd to rest my transient sorrows,
  Still'd my godless greed at last.

But my downward glance, returning,
   Shrank in fright from what it spy'd;
Slopes in hideous torment burning,
   Terror in the brooklet's tide:
For the dell, of shade denuded
   By my desecrating hand,
'Neath the bare sky blaz'd and brooded
   As a lost, accursed land.

FIRST PUBLISHED IN
The Tryout, March 1919

THE HOUSE

———————————

'Tis a grove-circled dwelling
    Set close to a hill,
Where the branches are telling
    Strange legends of ill;
Over timbers so old
    That they breathe of the dead,
Crawl the vines, green and cold,
    By strange nourishment fed;
And no man knows the juices they suck from the depths of
  their dank slimy bed.

In the gardens are growing
    Tall blossoms and fair,
Each pallid bloom throwing
    Perfume on the air;
But the afternoon sun
    With its shining red rays
Makes the picture loom dun
    On the curious gaze,
And above the sween scent of the the blossoms rise odours of
  numberless days.

The rank grasses are waving
    On terrace and lawn,
Dim memories sav'ring
    Of things that have gone;
The stones of the walks
    Are encrusted and wet,
And a strange spirit stalks
    When the red sun has set,
And the soul of the watcher is fill'd with faint pictures he fain
  would forget.

It was in the hot Junetime
    I stood by that scene,
When the gold rays of noontime
    Beat bright on the green.
But I shiver'd with cold,
    Groping feebly for light,
As a picture unroll'd—
    And my age-spanning sight
Saw the time I had been there before flash like fulgury out of
  the night.

FIRST PUBLISHED IN
National Enquirer, December 1919

84

THE CITY

It was golden and splendid,
    That City of light;
  A vision suspended
    In deeps of the night;
A region of wonder and glory, whose temples were marble and
  white.

  I remember the season
    It dawn'd on my gaze;
  The mad time of unreason,
    The brain-numbing days
When Winter, white-sheeted and ghastly, stalks onward to
  torture and craze.

  More lovely than Zion
    It shone in the sky,
  When the beams of Orion
    Beclouded my eye,
Bringing sleep that was fill'd with dim mem'ries of moments
  obscure and gone by.

  Its mansions were stately
    With carvings made fair,
  Each rising sedately
    On terraces rare,
And the gardens were fragrant and bright with strange miracles
  blossoming there.

The avenues lur'd me
With vistas sublime;
Tall arches assur'd me
That once on a time
I had wander'd in rapture beneath them, and bask'd in the
Halcyon clime.

On the plazas were standing
A sculptur'd array;
Long-bearded, commanding,
Grave men in their day—
But one stood dismantled and broken, its bearded face batter'd
away.

In that city effulgent
No mortal I saw;
But my fancy, indulgent
To memory's law,
Linger'd long on the forms in the plazas, and eyed their stone
features with awe.

I fann'd the faint ember
That glow'd in my mind,
And strove to remember
The aeons behind;
To rove thro' infinity freely, and visit the past unconfin'd.

Then the horrible warning
    Upon my soul sped
Like the ominous morning
    That rises in red,
And in panic I flew from the knowledge of terrors forgotten and
  dead.

First published in
The Vagrant, October 1919

TO
EDWARD JOHN
MORETON DRAX PLUNKETT

EIGHTEENTH BARON DUNSANY

As when the sun above a dusky wold
Springs into sight, and turns the gloom to gold,
Lights with his magic beams the dew-deck'd bow'rs,
And wakes to life the gay responsive flow'rs;
So now o'er realms where dark'ning dulness lies,
In solar state see shining *Plunkett* rise!
Monarch of Fancy! whose ethereal mind
Mounts fairy peaks, and leaves the throng behind;
Whose soul untainted bursts the bounds of space,
And leads to regions of supernal grace;
Can any praise thee with too strong a tone,
Who in this age of folly gleam'st alone?
Thy quill, *Dunsany*, with an art divine
Recalls the gods to each deserted shrine;
From mystic air a novel pantheon makes,
And with new spirits fills the meads and brakes;
With thee we wander thro' primeval bow'rs,
For thou hast brought earth's childhood back, and ours!
How leaps the soul, with sudden bliss increas'd,
When led by thee to lands beyond the East!
Sick of this sphere, in crime and conflict old,
We yearn for wonders distant and untold;
O'er Homer's page a second time we pore,
And rack our brains for gleams of infant lore:

But all in vain—for valiant tho' we strive
No common means these pictures can revive.
Then dawns *Dunsany* with celestial light,
And fulgent visions break upon our sight:
His barque enchanted each sad spirit bears
To shores of gold, beyond the reach of cares.
No earthly trammels now our thoughts may chain;
For childhood's fancy hath come back again!
What glitt'ring worlds now wait our eager eyes!
What roads untrodden beckon thro' the skies!
Wonders on wonders line the gorgeous ways,
And glorious vistas greet the ravish'd gaze;
Mountains of clouds, castles of crystal dreams,
Ethereal cities and Elysian streams;
Temples of blue, where myriad stars adore
Forgotten gods of aeons gone before!
Such are thine arts, *Dunsany*, such thy skill,
That scarce terrestrial seems thy moving quill;
Can man, and man alone, successful draw
Such scenes of wonder and domains of awe?
Our hearts, enraptur'd, fix thy mind's abode
In high *Pegāna*; hail thee as a god;
And sure, can aught more high or godlike be
Than such a fancy as resides in thee?
Delighted Pan a friend and peer perceives
As thy sweet music stirs the sylvan leaves;
The Nine, transported, bless thy golden lyre,
Approve thy fancy, and applaud thy fire;
Whilst Jove himself assumes a brother's tone,
And vows the pantheon equal to his own.
Dunsany, may thy days be glad and long;
Replete with visions, and atune with song;
May thy rare notes increasing millions cheer,
Thy name beloved, and thy mem'ry dear!
'Tis thou who hast in hours of dulness brought

New charms of language, and new gems of thought;
Hast with a poet's grace enrich'd the earth
With aureate dreams as noble as thy birth.
Grateful we name thee, bright with fix'd renown,
The fairest jewel in *Hibernia's* crown.

First published in
The Tryout, November 1919

THE
NIGHTMARE LAKE

———————————————

There is a lake in distant Zan,
Beyond the wonted haunts of man,
Where broods alone in a hideous state
A spirit dead and desolate;
A spirit ancient and unholy,
Heavy with fearsome melancholy,
Which from the waters dull and dense
Draws vapors cursed with pestilence.
Around the banks, a mire of clay,
Sprawl things offensive in decay,
And curious birds that reach that shore
Are seen by mortals nevermore.
Here shines by day the searing sun
On glassy wastes beheld by none,
And here by night pale moonbeams flow
Into the deeps that yawn below.
In nightmares only is it told
What scenes beneath those beams unfold;
What scenes, too old for human sight,
Lie sunken there in endless night;
For in those depths there only pace
The shadows of a voiceless race.
One midnight, redolent of ill,
I saw that lake, asleep and still;
While in the lurid sky there rode
A gibbous moon that glow'd and glow'd.
I saw the stretching marshy shore,

And the foul things those marshes bore:
Lizards and snakes convuls'd and dying;
Ravens and vampires putrefying;
All these, and hov'ring o'er the dead,
Narcophagi that on them fed.
And as the dreadful moon climb'd high,
Fright'ning the stars from out the sky,
I saw the lake's dull water glow
Till sunken things appear'd below.
There shone unnumber'd fathoms down,
The tow'rs of a forgotten town;
The tarnish'd domes and mossy walls;
Weed-tangled spires and empty halls;
Deserted fanes and vaults of dread,
And streets of gold uncoveted.
These I beheld, and saw beside
A horde of shapeless shadows glide;
A noxious horde which to my glance
Seem'd moving in a hideous dance
Round slimy sepulchres that lay
Beside a never-travell'd way.
Straight from those tombs a heaving rose
That vex'd the waters' dull repose,
While lethal shades of upper space
Howl'd at the moon's sardonic face.
Then sank the lake within its bed,
Suck'd down to caverns of the dead,
Till from the reeking, new-stript earth
Curl'd foetid fumes of noisome birth.
About the city, nigh uncover'd,
The monstrous dancing shadows hover'd,
When lo! there oped with sudden stir
The portal of each sepulchre!
No ear may learn, no tongue may tell
What nameless horror then befell.

I see that lake—that moon agrin—
That city and the *things* within—
Waking, I pray that on that shore
The nightmare lake may sink *no more*!

FIRST PUBLISHED IN
The Vagrant, December 1919

ON READING
LORD DUNSANY'S
BOOK OF WONDER

The hours of night unheeded fly,
   And in the grate the embers fade;
Vast shadows one by one pass by
   In silent daemon cavalcade.

But still the magic volume holds
   The raptur'd eye in realms apart,
And fulgent sorcery enfolds
   The willing mind and eager heart.

The lonely room no more is there—
   For to the sight in pomp appear
Temples and cities pois'd in air
   And blazing glories—sphere on sphere.

First published in
The Silver Clarion, March 1920

CHRISTMAS

The cottage hearth beams warm and bright,
   The candles gaily glow;
The stars emit a kinder light
   Above the drifted snow.

Down from the sky a magic steals
   To glad the passing year,
And belfries sing with joyous peals,
   For Christmastide is here!

FIRST PUBLISHED IN
The Tryout, November 1920

SIR THOMAS TRYOUT

Died Nov. 15, 1921

To the venerable cat of a quaint gentleman
in His Majesty's Province of ye Massachusetts-Bay,
who publishes an amateur magazine call'd *The Tryout*.

The autumn hearth is strangely cold
   Despite the leaping flame,
And all the cheer that shone of old
   Seems lessen'd, dull'd, and tame.

For on the rug where lately doz'd
   A small and furry form,
An empty space is now disclos'd,
   That no mere blaze can warm.

The frosty plain and woodland walk
   In equal sadness sigh
For one who may no longer stalk
   With sylvan hunter's eye.

And if as olden Grecians tell,
   Amidst the thickets deep
A host of fauns and dryads dwell,
   I know that they must weep.

Must weep when autumn twilight brings
    Its mem'ries quaint to view,
Of all the little playful things
    That TOM was wont to do.

So tho' the busy world may pass
    With ne'er a tearful sign
The tiny mound of struggling grass
    Beneath the garden vine,

There's many an eye that fills tonight,
    And many a pensive strain
That sounds for him who stole from sight
    In the November rain.

No sage can trace his soul's advance,
    Or say it lives at all,
For Death against our curious glance
    Has rear'd a mighty wall.

Yet tender Fancy fain would stray
    To fair Hesperian bow'rs,
Where TOM may always purr and play
    Amidst the sun and flow'rs.

FIRST PUBLISHED IN
The Tryout, December 1921

PROVIDENCE

Where bay and river tranquil blend,
  And leafy hillsides rise,
The spires of Providence ascend
  Against the ancient skies.

Here centuried domes of shining gold
  Salute the morning's glare,
While slanting gables, odd and old,
  Are scatter'd here and there.

And in the narrow winding ways
  That climb o'er slope and crest,
The magic of forgotten days
  May still be found to rest.

A fanlight's gleam, a knocker's blow,
  A glimpse of Georgian brick—
The sights and sounds of long ago
  Where fancies cluster thick.

A flight of steps with iron rail,
  A belfry looming tall,
A slender steeple, carv'd and pale,
  A moss-grown garden wall.

A hidden churchyard's crumbling proofs
   Of man's mortality,
A rotting wharf where gambrel roofs
   Keep watch above the sea.

Square and parade, whose walls have tower'd
   Full fifteen decades long
By cobbled ways 'mid trees embower'd,
   And slighted by the throng.

Stone bridges spanning languid streams,
   Houses perch'd on the hill,
And courts where mysteries and dreams
   The brooding spirit fill.

Steep alley steps by vines conceal'd,
   Where small-pan'd windows glow
At twilight on a bit of field
   That chance has left below.

My Providence! What airy hosts
   Turn still thy gilded vanes;
What winds of elf that with grey ghosts
   People thine ancient lanes!

The chimes of evening as of old
   Above thy valleys sound,
While thy stern fathers 'neath the mould
   Make blest thy sacred ground.

Thou dream'st beside the waters there,
   Unchang'd by cruel years;
A spirit from an age more fair
   That shines behind our tears.

Thy twinkling lights each night I see,
   Tho' time and space divide;
For thou art of the soul of me,
   And always at my side!

FIRST PUBLISHED IN
The Brooklynite, November 1924

THE CATS

Babels of blocks to the high heavens tow'ring,
  Flames of futility swirling below;
Poisonous fungi in brick and stone flow'ring,
  Lanterns that shudder and death-lights that glow.

Black monstrous bridges across oily rivers,
  Cobwebs of cable by nameless things spun;
Catacomb deeps whose dank chaos delivers
  Streams of live foetor, that rots in the sun.

Colour and splendour, disease and decaying,
  Shrieking and ringing and scrambling insane,
Rabbles exotic to stranger-gods praying,
  Jumbles of odour that stifle the brain.

Legions of cats from the alleys nocturnal,
  Howling and lean in the glare of the moon,
Screaming the future with mouthings infernal,
  Yelling the burden of Pluto's red rune.

Tall tow'rs and pyramids ivy'd and crumbling,
   Bats that swoop low in the weed-cumber'd streets;
Bleak broken bridges o'er rivers whose rumbling
   Joins with no voice as the thick tide retreats.

Belfries that blackly against the moon totter,
   Caverns whose mouths are by mosses effac'd,
And living to answer the wind and the water,
   Only the lean cats that howl in the waste!

FIRST PUBLISHED IN
February 1925

FESTIVAL

There is snow on the ground,
    And the valleys are cold,
  And a midnight profound
    Blackly squats o'er the wold;
But a light on the hilltops half-seen hints of feastings unhallow'd and
  old.

There is death in the clouds,
    There is fear in the night,
  For the dead in their shrouds
    Hail the sun's turning flight,
And chant wild in the woods as they dance round a Yule-altar fungous
  and white.

To no gale of earth's kind
    Sways the forest of oak,
  Where the sick boughs entwin'd
    By mad mistletoes choke,
For these pow'rs are the pow'rs of the dark, from the graves of the lost
  Druid-folk.

And mayst thou to such deeds
    Be an abbot and priest,
  Singing cannibal greeds
    At each devil-wrought feast,
And to all the incredulous world shewing dimly the sign of the beast.

FIRST PUBLISHED IN
December 1925

HALLOWE'EN IN A SUBURB

The steeples are white in the wild moonlight,
   And the trees have a silver glare;
Past the chimneys high see the vampires fly,
   And the harpies of upper air,
     That flutter and laugh and stare.

For the village dead to the moon outspread
   Never shone in the sunset's gleam,
But grew out of the deep that the dead years keep
   Where the rivers of madness stream
     Down the gulfs to a pit of dream.

A chill wind weaves thro' the rows of sheaves
   In the meadows that shimmer pale,
And comes to twine where the headstones shine
   And the ghouls of the churchyard wail
     For harvests that fly and fail.

Not a breath of the strange grey gods of change
   That tore from the past its own
Can quicken this hour, when a spectral pow'r
   Spreads sleep o'er the cosmic throne
     And looses the vast unknown.

So here again stretch the vale and plain
   That moons long-forgotten saw,
And the dead leap gay in the pallid ray,
   Sprung out of the tomb's black maw
     To shake all the world with awe.

And all that the morn shall greet forlorn,
   The ugliness and the pest
Of rows where thick rise the stones and brick,
   Shall some day be with the rest,
   And brood with the shades unblest.

Then wild in the dark let the lemurs bark,
   And the leprous spires ascend;
For new and old alike in the fold
   Of horror and death are penn'd,
   For the hounds of Time to rend.

FIRST PUBLISHED IN
The National Amateur, March 1926

THE WOOD

They cut it down, and where the pitch-black aisles
  Of forest night had hid eternal things,
They scal'd the sky with tow'rs and marble piles
  To make a city for their revellings.

White and amazing to the lands around
  That wondrous wealth of domes and turrets rose;
Crystal and ivory, sublimely crown'd
  With pinnacles that bore unmelting snows.

And through its halls the pipe and sistrum rang,
  While wine and riot brought their scarlet stains;
Never a voice of elder marvels sang,
  Nor any eye call'd up the hills and plains.

Thus down the years, till on one purple night
  A drunken minstrel in his careless verse
Spoke the vile words that should not see the light,
  And stirr'd the shadows of an ancient curse.

Forests may fall, but not the dusk they shield;
  So on the spot where that proud city stood,
The shuddering dawn no single stone reveal'd,
  But fled the blackness of a primal wood.

FIRST PUBLISHED IN
The Tryout, January 1929

THE OUTPOST

When evening cools the yellow stream,
　　And shadows stalk the jungle's ways,
　　Zimbabwe's palace flares ablaze
For a great King who fears to dream.

For he alone of all mankind
　　Waded the swamp that serpents shun;
　　And struggling toward the setting sun,
Came on the veldt that lies behind.

No other eyes had vented there
　　Since eyes were lent for human sight—
　　But there, as sunset turned to night,
He found the Elder Secret's lair.

Strange turrets rose beyond the plain,
　　And walls and bastions spread around
　　The distant domes that fouled the ground
Like leprous fungi after rain.

A grudging moon writhed up to shine
　　Past leagues where life can have no home;
　　And paling far-off tower and dome,
Shewed each unwindowed and malign.

Then he who in his boyhood ran
　　Through vine-hung ruins free of fear,
　　Trembled at what he saw—for here
Was no dead, ruined seat of man.

107

Inhuman shapes, half-seen, half-guessed,
  Half solid and half ether-spawned,
  Seethed down from starless voids that yawned
In heav'n, to these blank walls of pest.

And voidward from that pest-mad zone
  Amorphous hordes seethed darkly back,
  Their dim claws laden with the wrack
Of things that men have dreamed and known.

The ancient Fishers from Outside—
  Were there not tales the high-priest told,
  Of how they found the worlds of old,
And took what pelf their fancy spied?

Their hidden, dread-ringed outposts brood
  Upon a million worlds of space;
  Abhorred by every living race,
Yet scatheless in their solitude.

Sweating with fright, the watcher crept
  Back to the swamp that serpents shun,
  So that he lay, by rise of sun,
Safe in the palace where he slept.

None saw him leave, or come at dawn,
  Nor does his flesh bear any mark
  Of what he met in that curst dark—
Yet from his sleep all peace has gone.

When evening cools the yellow stream,
  And shadows stalk the jungle's ways,
  Zimbabwe's palace flares ablaze,
For a great King who fears to dream.

FIRST PUBLISHED IN
Bacon's Essays, Spring 1930

THE
ANCIENT TRACK

There was no hand to hold me back
That night I found the ancient track
Over the hill, and strained to see
The fields that teased my memory.
This tree, that wall—I knew them well,
And all the roofs and orchards fell
Familiarly upon my mind
As from a past not far behind.
I knew what shadows would be cast
When the late moon came up at last
From back of Zaman's Hill, and how
The vale would shine three hours from now.
And when the path grew steep and high,
And seemed to end against the sky,
I had no fear of what might rest
Beyond that silhouetted crest.
Straight on I walked, while all the night
Grew pale with phosphorescent light,
And wall and farmhouse gable glowed
Unearthly by the climbing road.
There was the milestone that I knew—
"Two miles to Dunwich"—now the view
Of distant spire and roofs would dawn
With ten more upward paces gone. . . .

There was no hand to hold me back
That night I found the ancient track,
And reached the crest to see outspread
A valley of the lost and dead:
And over Zaman's Hill the horn
Of a malignant moon was born,
To light the weeds and vines that grew
On ruined walls I never knew.
The fox-fire glowed in field and bog,
And unknown waters spewed a fog
Whose curling talons mocked the thought
That I had ever known this spot.
Too well I saw from the mad scene
That my loved past had never been—
Nor was I now upon the trail
Descending to that long-dead vale.
Around was fog—ahead, the spray
Of star-streams in the Milky Way. . . .
There was no hand to hold me back
That night I found the ancient track.

FIRST PUBLISHED
Weird Tales, March 1930

THE MESSENGER

To Bertrand K. Hart, Esq.

The thing, he said, would come that night at three
From the old churchyard on the hill below;
But crouching by an oak fire's wholesome glow,
I tried to tell myself it could not be.
Surely, I mused, it was a pleasantry
Devised by one who did not truly know
The Elder Sign, bequeathed from long ago,
That sets the fumbling forms of darkness free.

He had not meant it—no—but still I lit
Another lamp as starry Leo climbed
Out of the Seekonk, and a steeple chimed
Three—and the firelight faded, bit by bit.
Then at the door that cautious rattling came—
And the mad truth devoured me like a flame!

FIRST PUBLISHED
Weird Tales, July 1938

FUNGI
FROM YUGGOTH

I. THE BOOK

The place was dark and dusty and half-lost
In tangles of old alleys near the quays,
Reeking of strange things brought in from the seas,
And with queer curls of fog that west winds tossed.
Small lozenge panes, obscured by smoke and frost,
Just shewed the books, in piles like twisted trees,
Rotting from floor to roof—congeries
Of crumbling elder lore at little cost.

I entered, charmed, and from a cobwebbed heap
Took up the nearest tome and thumbed it through,
Trembling at curious words that seemed to keep
Some secret, monstrous if one only knew.
Then, looking for some seller old in craft,
I could find nothing but a voice that laughed.

II. PURSUIT

I held the book beneath my coat, at pains
To hide the thing from sight in such a place;
Hurrying through the ancient harbor lanes
With often-turning head and nervous pace.
Dull, furtive windows in old tottering brick
Peered at me oddly as I hastened by,

And thinking what they sheltered, I grew sick
For a redeeming glimpse of clean blue sky.

No one had seen me take the thing—but still
A blank laugh echoed in my whirling head,
And I could guess what nighted worlds of ill
Lurked in that volume I had coveted.
The way grew strange—the walls alike and madding—
And far behind me, unseen feet were padding.

III. THE KEY

I do not know what windings in the waste
Of those strange sea-lanes brought me home once more,
But on my porch I trembled, white with haste
To get inside and bolt the heavy door.
I had the book that told the hidden way
Across the void and through the space-hung screens
That hold the undimensioned worlds at bay,
And keep lost aeons to their own demesnes.

At last the key was mine to those vague visions
Of sunset spires and twilight woods that brood
Dim in the gulfs beyond this earth's precisions,
Lurking as memories of infinitude.
The key was mine, but as I sat there mumbling,
The attic window shook with a faint fumbling.

IV. RECOGNITION

The day had come again, when as a child
I saw—just once—that hollow of old oaks,
Grey with a ground-mist that enfolds and chokes

The slinking shapes which madness has defiled.
It was the same—an herbage rank and wild
Clings round an altar whose carved sign invokes
That Nameless One to whom a thousand smokes
Rose, aeons gone, from unclean towers up-piled.

I saw the body spread on that dank stone,
And knew those things which feasted were not men;
I knew this strange, grey world was not my own,
But Yuggoth, past the starry voids—and then
The body shrieked at me with a dead cry,
And all too late I knew that it was I!

V. HOMECOMING

The daemon said that he would take me home
To the pale, shadowy land I half recalled
As a high place of stair and terrace, walled
With marble balustrades that sky-winds comb,
While miles below a maze of dome on dome
And tower on tower beside a sea lies sprawled.
Once more, he told me, I would stand enthralled
On those old heights, and hear the far-off foam.

All this he promised, and through sunset's gate
He swept me, past the lapping lakes of flame,
And red-gold thrones of gods without a name
Who shriek in fear at some impending fate.
Then a black gulf with sea-sounds in the night:
"Here was your home," he mocked, "when you had sight!"

VI. THE LAMP

We found the lamp inside those hollow cliffs
Whose chiseled sign no priest in Thebes could read,
And from whose caverns frightened hieroglyphs
Warned every living creature of earth's breed.
No more was there—just that one brazen bowl
With traces of a curious oil within;
Fretted with some obscurely patterned scroll,
And symbols hinting vaguely of strange sin.

Little the fears of forty centuries meant
To us as we bore off our slender spoil,
And when we scanned it in our darkened tent
We struck a match to test the ancient oil.
It blazed—great God! . . . But the vast shapes we saw
In that mad flash have seared our lives with awe.

VII. ZAMAN'S HILL

The great hill hung close over the old town,
A precipice against the main street's end;
Green, tall, and wooded, looking darkly down
Upon the steeple at the highway bend.
Two hundred years the whispers had been heard
About what happened on the man-shunned slope—
Tales of an oddly mangled deer or bird,
Or of lost boys whose kin had ceased to hope.

One day the mail-man found no village there,
Nor were its folk or houses seen again;
People came out from Aylesbury to stare—
Yet they all told the mail-man it was plain

That he was mad for saying he had spied
The great hill's gluttonous eyes, and jaws stretched wide.

VIII. THE PORT

Ten miles from Arkham I had struck the trail
That rides the cliff-edge over Boynton Beach,
And hoped that just at sunset I could reach
The crest that looks on Innsmouth in the vale.
Far out at sea was a retreating sail,
White as hard years of ancient winds could bleach,
But evil with some portent beyond speech,
So that I did not wave my hand or hail.

Sails out of lnnsmouth! echoing old renown
Of long-dead times. But now a too-swift night
Is closing in, and I have reached the height
Whence I so often scan the distant town.
The spires and roofs are there—but look! The gloom
Sinks on dark lanes, as lightless as the tomb!

IX. THE COURTYARD

It was the city I had known before;
The ancient, leprous town where mongrel throngs
Chant to strange gods, and beat unhallowed gongs
In crypts beneath foul alleys near the shore.
The rotting, fish-eyed houses leered at me
From where they leaned, drunk and half-animate,
As edging through the filth I passed the gate
To the black courtyard where the man would be.

The dark walls closed me in, and loud I cursed
That ever I had come to such a den,
When suddenly a score of windows burst
Into wild light, and swarmed with dancing men:
Mad, soundless revels of the dragging dead—
And not a corpse had either hands or head!

X. THE PIGEON-FLYERS

They took me slumming, where gaunt walls of brick
Bulge outward with a viscous stored-up evil,
And twisted faces, thronging foul and thick,
Wink messages to alien god and devil.
A million fires were blazing in the streets,
And from flat roofs a furtive few would fly
Bedraggled birds into the yawning sky
While hidden drums droned on with measured beats.

I knew those fires were brewing monstrous things,
And that those birds of space had been *Outside*—
I guessed to what dark planet's crypts they plied,
And what they brought from Thog beneath their wings.
The others laughed—till struck too mute to speak
By what they glimpsed in one bird's evil beak.

XI. THE WELL

Farmer Seth Atwood was past eighty when
He tried to sink that deep well by his door,
With only Eb to help him bore and bore.
We laughed, and hoped he'd soon be sane again.
And yet, instead, young Eb went crazy, too,
So that they shipped him to the county farm.

Seth bricked the well-mouth up as tight as glue—
Then hacked an artery in his gnarled left arm.

After the funeral we felt bound to get
Out to that well and rip the bricks away,
But all we saw were iron hand-holds set
Down a black hole deeper than we could say.
And yet we put the bricks back—for we found
The hole too deep for any line to sound.

XII. THE HOWLER

They told me not to take the Briggs' Hill path
That used to be the highroad through to Zoar,
For Goody Watkins, hanged in seventeen-four,
Had left a certain monstrous aftermath.
Yet when I disobeyed, and had in view
The vine-hung cottage by the great rock slope,
I could not think of elms or hempen rope,
But wondered why the house still seemed so new.

Stopping a while to watch the fading day,
I heard faint howls, as from a room upstairs,
When through the ivied panes one sunset ray
Struck in, and caught the howler unawares.
I glimpsed—and ran in frenzy from the place,
And from a four-pawed thing with human face.

XIII. HESPERIA

The winter sunset, flaming beyond spires
And chimneys half-detached from this dull sphere,
Opens great gates to some forgotten year

Of elder splendours and divine desires.
Expectant wonders burn in those rich fires,
Adventure-fraught, and not untinged with fear;
A row of sphinxes where the way leads clear
Toward walls and turrets quivering to far lyres.

It is the land where beauty's meaning flowers;
Where every unplaced memory has a source;
Where the great river Time begins its course
Down the vast void in starlit streams of hours.
Dreams bring us close—but ancient lore repeats
That human tread has never soiled these streets.

XIV. STAR-WINDS

It is a certain hour of twilight glooms,
Mostly in autumn, when the star-wind pours
Down hilltop streets, deserted out-of-doors,
But shewing early lamplight from snug rooms.
The dead leaves rush in strange, fantastic twists,
And chimney-smoke whirls round with alien grace,
Heeding geometries of outer space,
While Fomalhaut peers in through southward mists.

This is the hour when moonstruck poets know
What fungi sprout in Yuggoth, and what scents
And tints of flowers fill Nithon's continents,
Such as in no poor earthly garden blow.
Yet for each dream these winds to us convey,
A dozen more of ours they sweep away!

XV. ANTARKTOS

Deep in my dream the great bird whispered queerly
Of the black cone amid the polar waste;
Pushing above the ice-sheet lone and drearly,
By storm-crazed aeons battered and defaced.
Hither no living earth-shapes take their courses,
And only pale auroras and faint suns
Glow on that pitted rock, whose primal sources
Are guessed at dimly by the Elder Ones.

If men should glimpse it, they would merely wonder
What tricky mound of Nature's build they spied;
But the bird told of vaster parts, that under
The mile-deep ice-shroud crouch and brood and bide.
God help the dreamer whose mad visions shew
Those dead eyes set in crystal gulfs below!

XVI. THE WINDOW

The house was old, with tangled wings outthrown,
Of which no one could ever half keep track,
And in a small room somewhat near the back
Was an odd window sealed with ancient stone.
There, in a dream-plagued childhood, quite alone
I used to go, where night reigned vague and black;
Parting the cobwebs with a curious lack
Of fear, and with a wonder each time grown.

One later day I brought the masons there
To find what view my dim forbears had shunned,
But as they pierced the stone, a rush of air
Burst from the alien voids that yawned beyond.

They fled—but I peered through and found unrolled
All the wild worlds of which my dreams had told.

XVII. A MEMORY

There were great steppes, and rocky table-lands
Stretching half-limitless in starlit night,
With alien campfires shedding feeble light
On beasts with tinkling bells, in shaggy bands.
Far to the south the plain sloped low and wide
To a dark zigzag line of wall that lay
Like a huge python of some primal day
Which endless time had chilled and petrified.

I shivered oddly in the cold, thin air,
And wondered where I was and how I came,
When a cloaked form against a campfire's glare
Rose and approached, and called me by my name.
Staring at that dead face beneath the hood,
I ceased to hope—because I understood.

XVIII. THE GARDENS OF YIN

Beyond that wall, whose ancient masonry
Reached almost to the sky in moss-thick towers,
There would be terraced gardens, rich with flowers,
And flutter of bird and butterfly and bee.
There would be walks, and bridges arching over
Warm lotos-pools reflecting temple eaves,
And cherry-trees with delicate boughs and leaves
Against a pink sky where the herons hover.

All would be there, for had not old dreams flung
Open the gate to that stone-lanterned maze
Where drowsy streams spin out their winding ways,
Trailed by green vines from bending branches hung?
I hurried—but when the wall rose, grim and great,
I found there was no longer any gate.

XIX. THE BELLS

Year after year I heard that faint, far ringing
Of deep-toned bells on the black midnight wind;
Peals from no steeple I could ever find,
But strange, as if across some great void winging.
I searched my dreams and memories for a clue,
And thought of all the chimes my visions carried;
Of quiet Innsmouth, where the white gulls tarried
Around an ancient spire that once I knew.

Always perplexed I heard those far notes falling,
Till one March night the bleak rain splashing cold
Beckoned me back through gateways of recalling
To elder towers where the mad clappers tolled.
They tolled—but from the sunless tides that pour
Through sunken valleys on the sea's dead floor.

XX. NIGHT-GAUNTS

Out of what crypt they crawl, I cannot tell,
But every night I see the rubbery things,
Black, horned, and slender, with membraneous wings,
And tails that bear the bifid barb of hell.
They come in legions on the north wind's swell,
With obscene clutch that titillates and stings,

Snatching me off on monstrous voyagings
To grey worlds hidden deep in nightmare's well.

Over the jagged peaks of Thok they sweep,
Heedless of all the cries I try to make,
And down the nether pits to that foul lake
Where the puffed shoggoths splash in doubtful sleep.
But oh! If only they would make some sound,
Or wear a face where faces should be found!

XXI. NYARLATHOTEP

And at the last from inner Egypt came
The strange dark One to whom the fellahs bowed;
Silent and lean and cryptically proud,
And wrapped in fabrics red as sunset flame.
Throngs pressed around, frantic for his commands,
But leaving, could not tell what they had heard;
While through the nations spread the awestruck word
That wild beasts followed him and licked his hands.

Soon from the sea a noxious birth began;
Forgotten lands with weedy spires of gold;
The ground was cleft, and mad auroras rolled
Down on the quaking citadels of man.
Then, crushing what he chanced to mould in play,
The idiot Chaos blew Earth's dust away.

XXII. AZATHOTH

Out in the mindless void the daemon bore me,
Past the bright clusters of dimensioned space,
Till neither time nor matter stretched before me,

But only Chaos, without form or place.
Here the vast Lord of All in darkness muttered
Things he had dreamed but could not understand,
While near him shapeless bat-things flopped and fluttered
In idiot vortices that ray-streams fanned.

They danced insanely to the high, thin whining
Of a cracked flute clutched in a monstrous paw,
Whence flow the aimless waves whose chance combining
Gives each frail cosmos its eternal law.
"I am His Messenger," the daemon said,
As in contempt he struck his Master's head.

XXIII. MIRAGE

I do not know if ever it existed—
That lost world floating dimly on Time's stream—
And yet I see it often, violet-misted,
And shimmering at the back of some vague dream.
There were strange towers and curious lapping rivers,
Labyrinths of wonder, and low vaults of light,
And bough-crossed skies of flame, like that which quivers
Wistfully just before a winter's night.

Great moors led off to sedgy shores unpeopled,
Where vast birds wheeled, while on a windswept hill
There was a village, ancient and white-steepled,
With evening chimes for which I listen still.
I do not know what land it is—or dare
Ask when or why I was, or will be, there.

XXIV. THE CANAL

Somewhere in dream there is an evil place
Where tall, deserted buildings crowd along
A deep, black, narrow channel, reeking strong
Of frightful things whence oily currents race.
Lanes with old walls half meeting overhead
Wind off to streets one may or may not know,
And feeble moonlight sheds a spectral glow
Over long rows of windows, dark and dead.

There are no footfalls, and the one soft sound
Is of the oily water as it glides
Under stone bridges, and along the sides
Of its deep flume, to some vague ocean bound.
None lives to tell when that stream washed away
Its dream-lost region from the world of clay.

XXV. ST. TOAD'S

"Beware St. Toad's cracked chimes!" I heard him scream
As I plunged into those mad lanes that wind
In labyrinths obscure and undefined
South of the river where old centuries dream.
He was a furtive figure, bent and ragged,
And in a flash had staggered out of sight,
So still I burrowed onward in the night
Toward where more roof-lines rose, malign and jagged.

No guide-book told of what was lurking here—
But now I heard another old man shriek:
"Beware St.Toad's cracked chimes!" And growing weak,
I paused, when a third greybeard croaked in fear:

126

"Beware St. Toad's cracked chimes!" Aghast, I fled—
Till suddenly that black spire loomed ahead.

XXVI. THE FAMILIARS

John Whateley lived about a mile from town,
Up where the hills began to huddle thick;
We never thought his wits were very quick,
Seeing the way he let his farm run down.
He used to waste his time on some queer books
He'd found around the attic of his place,
Till funny lines got creased into his face,
And folks all said they didn't like his looks.

When he began those night-howls we declared
He'd better be locked up away from harm,
So three men from the Aylesbury town farm
Went for him—but came back alone and scared.
They'd found him talking to two crouching things
That at their step flew off on great black wings.

XXVII. THE ELDER PHAROS

From Leng, where rocky peaks climb bleak and bare
Under cold stars obscure to human sight,
There shoots at dusk a single beam of light
Whose far blue rays make shepherds whine in prayer.
They say (though none has been there) that it comes
Out of a pharos in a tower of stone,
Where the last Elder One lives on alone,
Talking to Chaos with the beat of drums.

The Thing, they whisper, wears a silken mask
Of yellow, whose queer folds appear to hide
A face not of this earth, though none dares ask
Just what those features are, which bulge inside.
Many, in man's first youth, sought out that glow,
But what they found, no one will ever know.

XXVIII. EXPECTANCY

I cannot tell why some things hold for me
A sense of unplumbed marvels to befall,
Or of a rift in the horizon's wall
Opening to worlds where only gods can be.
There is a breathless, vague expectancy,
As of vast ancient pomps I half recall,
Or wild adventures, uncorporeal,
Ecstasy-fraught, and as a day-dream free.

It is in sunsets and strange city spires,
Old villages and woods and misty downs,
South winds, the sea, low hills, and lighted towns,
Old gardens, half-heard songs, and the moon's fires.
But though its lure alone makes life worth living,
None gains or guesses what it hints at giving.

XXIX. NOSTALGIA

Once every year, in autumn's wistful glow,
The birds fly out over an ocean waste,
Calling and chattering in a joyous haste
To reach some land their inner memories know.
Great terraced gardens where bright blossoms blow,
And lines of mangoes luscious to the taste,

And temple-groves with branches interlaced
Over cool paths—all these their vague dreams shew.

They search the sea for marks of their old shore—
For the tall city, white and turreted—
But only empty waters stretch ahead,
So that at last they turn away once more.
Yet sunken deep where alien polyps throng,
The old towers miss their lost, remembered song.

XXX. BACKGROUND

I never can be tied to raw, new things,
For I first saw the light in an old town,
Where from my window huddled roofs sloped down
To a quaint harbour rich with visionings.
Streets with carved doorways where the sunset beams
Flooded old fanlights and small window-panes,
And Georgian steeples topped with gilded vanes—
These were the sights that shaped my childhood dreams.

Such treasures, left from times of cautious leaven,
Cannot but loose the hold of flimsier wraiths
That flit with shifting ways and muddled faiths
Across the changeless walls of earth and heaven.
They cut the moment's thongs and leave me free
To stand alone before eternity.

XXXI. THE DWELLER

It had been old when Babylon was new;
None knows how long it slept beneath that mound,
Where in the end our questing shovels found
Its granite blocks and brought it back to view.
There were vast pavements and foundation-walls,
And crumbling slabs and statues, carved to shew
Fantastic beings of some long ago
Past anything the world of man recalls.

And then we saw those stone steps leading down
Through a choked gate of graven dolomite
To some black haven of eternal night
Where elder signs and primal secrets frown.
We cleared a path—but raced in mad retreat
When from below we heard those clumping feet.

XXXII. ALIENATION

His solid flesh had never been away,
For each dawn found him in his usual place,
But every night his spirit loved to race
Through gulfs and worlds remote from common day.
He had seen Yaddith, yet retained his mind,
And come back safely from the Ghooric zone,
When one still night across curved space was thrown
That beckoning piping from the voids behind.

He waked that morning as an older man,
And nothing since has looked the same to him.
Objects around float nebulous and dim—
False, phantom trifles of some vaster plan.

His folk and friends are now an alien throng
To which he struggles vainly to belong.

XXXIII. HARBOUR WHISTLES

Over old roofs and past decaying spires
The harbour whistles chant all through the night;
Throats from strange ports, and beaches far and white,
And fabulous oceans, ranged in motley choirs.
Each to the other alien and unknown,
Yet all, by some obscurely focussed force
From brooding gulfs beyond the Zodiac's course,
Fused into one mysterious cosmic drone.

Through shadowy dreams they send a marching line
Of still more shadowy shapes and hints and views;
Echoes from outer voids, and subtle clues
To things which they themselves cannot define.
And always in that chorus, faintly blent,
We catch some notes no earth-ship ever sent.

XXXIV. RECAPTURE

The way led down a dark, half-wooded heath
Where moss-grey boulders humped above the mould,
And curious drops, disquieting and cold,
Sprayed up from unseen streams in gulfs beneath.
There was no wind, nor any trace of sound
In puzzling shrub, or alien-featured tree,
Nor any view before—till suddenly,
Straight in my path, I saw a monstrous mound.

Half to the sky those steep sides loomed upspread,
Rank-grassed, and cluttered by a crumbling flight
Of lava stairs that scaled the fear-topped height
In steps too vast for any human tread.
I shrieked—and *knew* what primal star and year
Had sucked me back from man's dream-transient sphere!

XXXV. EVENING STAR

I saw it from that hidden, silent place
Where the old wood half shuts the meadow in.
It shone through all the sunset's glories—thin
At first, but with a slowly brightening face.
Night came, and that lone beacon, amber-hued,
Beat on my sight as never it did of old;
The evening star—but grown a thousandfold
More haunting in this hush and solitude.

It traced strange pictures on the quivering air—
Half-memories that had always filled my eyes—
Vast towers and gardens; curious seas and skies
Of some dim life—I never could tell where.
But now I knew that through the cosmic dome
Those rays were calling from my far, lost home.

XXXVI. CONTINUITY

There is in certain ancient things a trace
Of some dim essence—more than form or weight;
A tenuous aether, indeterminate,
Yet linked with all the laws of time and space.
A faint, veiled sign of continuities
That outward eyes can never quite descry;

Of locked dimensions harbouring years gone by,
And out of reach except for hidden keys.

It moves me most when slanting sunbeams glow
On old farm buildings set against a hill,
And paint with life the shapes which linger still
From centuries less a dream than this we know.
In that strange light I feel I am not far
From the fixt mass whose sides the ages are.

FIRST PUBLISHED IN
December 1929

[LITTLE SAM PERKINS]

The ancient garden seems tonight
  A deeper gloom to bear,
As if some silent shadow's blight
  Were hov'ing in the air.

With hidden griefs the grasses sway,
  Unable quite to word them—
Remembering from yesterday
  The little paws that stirr'd them.

FIRST PUBLISHED IN
Olympian, Autumn 1940

DEAD PASSION'S FLAME

A POEM BY BLANK FRAILTY

Ah, Passion, like a voice—that buds!
With many thorns . . . that sharply stick:
Recalls to me the longing of our bloods . . .
And—makes my wearied heart requick! . . . .

FIRST PUBLISHED IN
Summer 1935

ARCADIA

BY HEAD BALLEDUP

O give me the life of the village,
   Uninhibited, free, and sweet;
The place where the arts all flourish,
   Grove Court and Christopher Street.

I am sick of the old conventions,
   And critics who will not praise,
So sing ho for the open spaces,
   And aesthetes with kindly ways.

Here every bard is a genius,
   And artists are Raphaels,
And above the roofs of Patchin Place
   The Muse of Talent dwells.

FIRST PUBLISHED IN
Summer 1935

IN A SEQUESTER'D PROVIDENCE CHURCHYARD WHERE ONCE POE WALK'D

Eternal brood the shadows on this ground,
Dreaming of centuries that have gone before;
Great elms rise solemnly by slab and mound,
Arch'd high above a hidden world of yore.
Round all the scene a light of memory plays,
And dead leaves whisper of departed days,
Longing for sights and sounds that are no more.

Lonely and sad, a spectre glides along
Aisles where of old his living footsteps fell;
No common glance discerns him, tho' his song
Peals down thro' time with a mysterious spell:
Only the few who sorcery's secret know
Espy amidst these tombs the shade of Poe.

First published in
August 1936

NATHICANA

It was in the pale garden of Zaïs;
The mist-shrouded gardens of Zaïs,
Where blossoms the white nephalotë,
The redolent herald of midnight.
There slumber the still lakes of crystal,
And streamlets that flow without murm'ring;
Smooth streamlets from caverns of Kathos
Where brood the calm spirits of twilight.
And over the lakes and the streamlets
Are bridges of pure alabaster,
White bridges all cunningly carven
With figures of fairies and daemons.
Here glimmer strange suns and strange planets,
And strange is the crescent Banapis
That sets 'yond the ivy-grown ramparts
Where thickens the dust of the evening.
Here fall the white vapours of Yabon;
And here in the swirl of vapours
I saw the divine Nathicana;
The garlanded, white Nathicana;
The slender, black-hair'd Nathicana;
The sloe-ey'd, red-lipp'd Nathicana;
The silver-voic'd, sweet Nathicana;
The pale-rob'd, belov'd Nathicana.
And ever was she my belovèd,
From ages when Time was unfashion'd;
From days when the stars were not fashion'd

Nor any thing fashion'd but Yabon.
And here dwelt we ever and ever,
The innocent children of Zaïs,
At peace in the paths and the arbours,
White-crown'd with the blest nephalotë.
How oft would we float in the twilight
O'er flow'r-cover'd pastures and hillsides
All white with the lowly astalthon;
The lowly yet lovely astalthon,
And dream in a world made of dreaming
The dreams that are fairer than Aidenn;
Bright dreams that are truer than reason!
So dream'd and so lov'd we thro' ages,
Till came the curs'd season of Dzannin;
The daemon-damn'd season of Dzannin;
When red shone the suns and the planets,
And red gleamed the crescent Banapis,
And red fell the vapours of Yabon.
Then redden'd the blossoms and streamlets
And lakes that lay under the bridges,
And even the calm alabaster
Glow'd pink with uncanny reflections
Till all the carv'd fairies and daemons
Leer'd redly from the backgrounds of shadow.
Now redden'd my vision, and madly
I strove to peer thro' the dense curtain
And glimpse the divine Nathicana;
The pure, ever-pale Nathicana;
The lov'd, the unchang'd Nathicana.
But vortex on vortex of madness
Beclouded my labouring vision;
My damnable, reddening vision
That built a new world for my seeing;

A new world of redness and darkness,
A horrible coma call'd living.
So now in this coma call'd living
I view the bright phantons of beauty;
The false, hollow phantoms of beauty
That cloak all the evils of Dzannin.
I view them with infinite longing,
So like do they seem to my lov'd one;
So shapely and fair like my lov'd one;
Yet foul from their eyes shines their evil;
Their cruel and pitiless evil,
More evil than Thaphron and Latgoz,
Twice ill for its gorgeous concealment.
And only in slumbers of midnight
Appears the lost maid Nathicana,
The pallid, the pure Nathicana,
Who fades at the glance of the dreamer.
Again and again do I seek her;
I woo with deep draughts of Plathotis,
Deep draughts brew'd in wine of Astarte
And strengthen'd with tears of long weeping.
I yearn for the gardens of Zaïs;
The lovely lost garden of Zaïs
Where blossoms the white nephalotë,
The redolent herald of midnight.
The last potent draught I am brewing;
A draught that the daemons delight in;
A draught that will banish the redness;
The horrible coma call'd living.
Soon, soon, if I fail not in brewing,
The redness and madness will vanish,
And deep in the worm-peopled darkness
Will rot the base chains that hav bound me.

Once more shall the gardens of Zaïs
Dawn white on my long-tortur'd vision,
And there midst the vapours of Yabon
Will stand the divine Nathicana;
The deathless, restor'd Nathicana
Whose like is not met with in living.

FIRST PUBLISHED IN
The Vagrant, Spring 1927

A CYCLE OF VERSE

I. OCEANUS

Sometimes I stand upon the shore
Where ocean vaults their effluence pour,
And troubled waters sigh and shriek
Of secrets that they dare not speak.
From nameless valleys far below,
And hills and plains no man may know,
The mystic swells and sullen surges
Hint like accursed thaumaturges
A thousand horrors, big with awe,
That forgotten ages saw.
O salt, salt winds, that bleakly sweep
Across the barren heaving deep;
O wild, wan waves, that call to mind
The chaos Earth hath left behind;
Of you I ask one thing alone—
Leave, leave your ancient lore unknown!

II. CLOUDS

Of late I climb'd a lonely height
And watch'd the moon-streak'd clouds in flight,
Whose forms fantastic reel'd and whirl'd
Like genii of a spectral world.
Thin cirri veil'd the silv'ry dome
And waver'd like the ocean foam,

While shapes of darker, heavier kind
Scudded before a daemon wind.
Methought the churning vapours took
Now and anon a fearsome look,
As if amidst the fog and blur
March'd figures known and sinister.
From west to east the things advanc'd—
A mocking train that leap'd and danc'd
Like Bacchanals with joined hands
In endless file thro' airy lands.
Aerial mutt'rings, dimly heard,
The comfort of my spirit stirr'd
With hideous thoughts, that bade me screen
My sight form the portentous scene.
"Yon fleeing mists," the murmurs said,
"Are ghosts of hopes, deny'd and dead."

III. MOTHER EARTH

One night I wander'd down the bank
Of a deep valley, hush'd and dank,
Whose stagnant air possess'd a taint
And chill that made me sick and faint.
The frequent trees on ev'ry hand
Loom'd like a ghastly goblin band,
And branches 'gainst the narrowing sky
Took shapes I fear'd—I knew not why.
Deeper I plung'd, and seem'd to grope
For some lost thing as joy or hope,
Yet found, for all my searchings there,
Naught save the phantoms of despair.
The walls contracted as I went
Still farther in my mad descent,
Till soon, of moon and stars bereft,

I crouch'd within a rocky cleft
So deep and ancient that the stone
Breath'd things primordial and unknown.
My hands, exploring, strove to trace
The features of the valley's face,
When midst the gloom they seem'd to find
An outline frightful to my mind.
Not any shape my straining eyes,
Could they have seen, might recognize;
For what I touch'd bespoke a day
Too old for man's fugacious sway.
The clinging lichens moist and hoary
Forbade me read the antique story;
But hidden water, trickling low,
Whisper'd the tales I should not know.

"Mortal, ephemeral and bold,
In mercy keep what I have told,
Yet think sometimes of what hath been,
And sights these crumbling rocks have seen;
Of sentience old ere thy weak brook
Appear'd in lesser magnitude,
And living things that yet servive,
Tho' not to human ken alive.
I AM THE VOICE OF MOTHER EARTH,
FROM WHENCE ALL HORRORS
HAVE THEIR BIRTH."

First published in 1918

Ingram Content Group UK Ltd.
Milton Keynes UK
UKHW012012100423
419951UK00003B/47

WALKING
FOR MIND,
BODY AND
SOUL

WALKING FOR MIND, BODY AND SOUL

Text by Jayne Hardy

An Hachette UK Company
www.hachette.co.uk

Vie Books, an imprint of Summersdale Publishers
Part of Octopus Publishing Group Limited
Carmelite House
50 Victoria Embankment
LONDON
EC4Y 0DZ
UK

www.summersdale.com

The authorized representative in the EEA is Hachette Ireland, 8 Castlecourt Centre, Dublin 15, D15 XTP3, Ireland (email: info@hbgi.ie)

Printed and bound in China

ISBN: 978-1-83799-516-5

This FSC® label means that materials used for the product have been responsibly sourced

Substantial discounts on bulk quantities of Summersdale books are available to corporations, professional associations and other organizations. For details contact general enquiries: telephone: +44 (0) 1243 771107 or email: enquiries@summersdale.com.

Neither the author nor the publisher can be held responsible for any injury, loss or claim – be it health, financial or otherwise – arising out of the use, or misuse, of the suggestions made herein. Always consult your doctor before trying any new form of exercise if you have a medical or health condition, or are worried about any of the side effects. This book is not intended as a substitute for the medical advice of a doctor or physician.

WALKING
FOR MIND,
BODY AND
SOUL

*How to Walk Your
Way to Wellness*

ROWAN BAILEY

vie

CONTENTS

INTRODUCTION

Walking is a humble yet profound activity that we often take for granted. We walk from here to there, without having to think about how we move around and usually without making the most of the journey, however short. Taking a walk isn't just about putting one foot in front of the other; it opens the door to a magical world that exists in plain sight. A world that shows us what it means to be truly alive. One where time slows and our innerness glows.

In the midst of our busy lives, walking is a precious gift. It offers us the chance to slow down, to breathe, to be present, and to reconnect with ourselves and our surroundings, helping us to understand that it truly is the journey that matters.

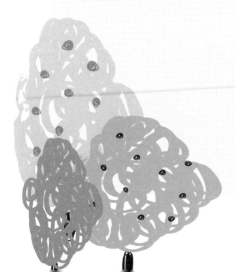

No two walks are ever the same. For not only do we find a new piece of ourselves in each step, but nature also unveils a piece of herself too. Through walking, we become attuned to the subtle nuances of the world around us, finding beauty in the simplest of moments.

Within this book, you'll learn that walking is not just exercise for the body – it's nourishment for the soul and the senses. You'll discover ideas, projects and activities which will foster creativity, imagination and play. You'll uncover tools and techniques on ways to engage your senses and how to use these to find calm. You'll find ways to unlock the transformative power of walking, leaving you with a mighty pep in your step.

Part One:
WALKING FOR PHYSICAL WELL-BEING

When our body is functioning well, it's easy to take it for granted and overlook its crucial role in allowing us to go about our days. Yet, the moment we experience any injury or discomfort, we're reminded of the importance of our physical health and how, when it's compromised, so too is our quality of life.

Recognizing the intrinsic connection between physical health and mental health underscores the significance of taking care of our bodies. When we do, we're investing in our future selves and the benefits are huge. Not only are we likely to live longer, but it'll also be a healthier and happier life, where we feel strong, supple and resilient. Taking care of our body means our body can take care of us.

Walking provides a great general workout, exercising muscles all round the body. The steady act of putting one foot in front of the other, transferring our weight and swinging our arms as we propel our body forward can improve heart health, strengthen our bones, lower blood pressure, burn calories and boost immunity.

Walking regularly helps us to achieve all of that and gives so much more. So step outside and let the world be your gym, your sanctuary and your playground.

WALKING IS THE BEST FORM OF EXERCISE

Forget running, lifting weights and jazzy exercise classes – walking has been hailed the best form of exercise around and it's not difficult to see why.

For starters, walking doesn't require any special kit or equipment, which immediately removes any financial barriers. It's a low-impact activity, making it accessible to people of all ages and fitness levels, as well as those with pre-existing medical conditions which could prevent them from participating in more strenuous forms of exercise. Yet it's still effective, because it engages multiple muscle groups – including the legs, core and arms – while also improving cardiovascular fitness and endurance. Best of all, it can be enjoyed year-round, anywhere in the world, wherever you are.

The guidelines recommend that we walk briskly for 150 minutes per week. That sounds like a lot but it's incredibly easy to incorporate walking into daily life. We can opt to take the stairs instead of the lift, walk short journeys instead of driving, take a walking break during our lunch hour or get off the bus a few stops early.

STRONG BONES AND HEALTHY JOINTS

Most people aren't aware that as we age, our bones weaken and lose their density, causing us to become frail and at higher risk of fractures and osteoporosis. Walking is a weight-bearing exercise, which means we're putting weight on our bones every step we take. Over time, this strengthens our bones, keeps them healthy and slows the loss of density. To get the best results, we want to aim to walk at a brisk pace for a mile (or 1.5 kilometres) a day.

More and more of us lead sedentary lives: working from home, spending an increasing amount of time sitting at desks or lounging on our sofas. Walking involves moving our joints, which can help to lubricate them and keep them supple. It also strengthens the muscles around the joints, providing extra support and stability.

Too much sitting can wreak havoc with our posture, causing rounded shoulders and an arched neck. Walking stretches out our spine and engages our core muscles. Over time, this helps to improve overall posture, reducing the risk of back pain and other issues.

BUILD MUSCLE

Walking may not have us bench-pressing our body weight to deadlift like a pro, but don't underestimate its power to build strength. When we walk, we engage a multitude of muscles throughout our body, including those in the legs, hips, core – and even our arms, if we're swinging them with purpose. The consistent use of the whole body during walking leads to increased strength and endurance.

Unlike when we "pump iron" at the gym, our muscles won't get bulky and bulgy from walking. Instead, we'll develop lean muscle tone and definition, particularly in the lower body. As we stride along, our leg muscles – including the quadriceps, hamstrings, calves and glutes – all come into play, working to propel us forward and support our body weight with each step.

If we wanted to up the ante, somewhat, we could incorporate hillwalking. Walking uphill requires greater effort from the lower body muscles as they work harder to lift the body against gravity. This helps to build muscular strength and endurance more effectively than walking on flat terrain.

Another way to enhance the impact of walking on strength is by including some weighted walking into our routine. This can be achieved by wearing a weighted vest or carrying handheld weights while walking. The additional resistance increases the workload on the muscles, leading to greater strength gains over time. However, it's important to start light and gradually increase the load to avoid strain or injury.

Always remember to listen to your body: start slowly, and progress at a pace that feels comfortable and sustainable for you.

We live in a fast-paced society.

Walking slows us down.

ROBERT SWEETGALL

Walking is not merely

a physical exercise;

it is a metaphor for life,

with its ups and downs,

twists and turns

BOOST METABOLISM
and burn calories

You might be surprised at just how effective walking can be in burning calories. Even a moderately paced walk for just 30 minutes can burn away 150 calories. That's the equivalent of a small bag of crisps, a couple of biscuits or a large banana. The more strenuous a walk in terms of pace, distance and inclination, the more calories we will burn.

A 2015 study also found that walking can help control our cravings. They discovered that a moderate-intensity 15-minute walk releases endorphins which significantly reduce cravings for high-calorie sugary snacks. This is particularly beneficial for those of us who tend to reach for that tub of ice cream or bar of chocolate when we're feeling stressed. Instead, we can lace up our shoes and, quite literally, walk off the craving.

That said, the benefits go far beyond just cravings and calorie burn. Walking has a fantastic impact on metabolic health too, particularly in improving insulin sensitivity. Our metabolism is a series of complex biochemical processes which determine our ability to use the food and drink we consume as fuel and turn it into cellular energy. By enhancing the body's ability to utilize insulin effectively, walking helps to keep blood sugar levels in check and reduces the risk of metabolic issues like type 2 diabetes.

IMPROVE DIGESTION
and gut health

The phrase "daily constitutional" is an old-fashioned term that was batted around by the upper classes in days long gone. This habit of going for a daily walk to restore or maintain good health was acknowledged to be helpful because of the positive effect it had on the digestive system. For want of a better term, it "got things moving".

Walking after a meal, especially a large one that has left us feeling sluggish and bloated, can be particularly supportive to our digestive system, speeding up the time it takes food to move from the stomach to the intestines. Taking a walk can reduce the likelihood of indigestion, heartburn, gas, constipation and bloating.

Additionally, each of us has a gut microbiome that is home to trillions of microbes: bacteria which reside in our digestive tract. The more diverse the microbes, the better it is for our immune function, brain, heart, nutrition absorption and digestive system. Walking increases the diversity of all those health-promoting microbes.

THE "SUNSHINE" VITAMIN: VITAMIN D

A positive side effect of all this walking outdoors is the increased exposure to sunlight and, therefore, vitamin D. Sunlight exposure triggers the synthesis of vitamin D, when sunrays touch our skin. However, during the winter months, when the days are shorter and the weather is often cloudy, it's easy to become deficient and it's advised we consider supplementation. During summer, spending 20 minutes outside should be enough to boost our vitamin D levels, and it really is worth the time and effort.

Vitamin D is essential for:

- Regulating calcium and phosphorus in the body
- Keeping our bones and teeth healthy and strong
- Reducing muscle pain and weakness
- A robust immune system, which protects us from infection and disease
- Regulating our mood and reducing the risk of depression
- Preventing hair loss

BOOST YOUR IMMUNE SYSTEM

Walking keeps us in good health in a variety of ways – not least because of the role it plays in bolstering our body's immune system, making us more resilient to infections and illnesses.

There are a few ways walking helps to keep us well:

Promotes circulation

As we walk, our heart rate increases and blood flow improves throughout the body, including to our vital organs and immune cells. The latter can then travel more efficiently to identify and combat pathogens.

Stimulates our lymphatic system

The lymphatic system is responsible for transporting lymph – a fluid containing white blood cells and other immune cells – throughout the body. By increasing lymphatic flow, walking helps to remove toxins and waste products from tissues.

Reduces inflammation in the body

Chronic inflammation has been linked to various health conditions, including autoimmune diseases and infections. Walking helps to regulate inflammation levels, promoting a balanced immune response.

Reduces stress levels

High levels of stress can weaken the immune system, making us more susceptible to infections. Walking provides an opportunity to clear the mind, reduce tension and promote relaxation, thereby supporting a healthy immune system.

*I was no longer
following a trail.
I was learning
to follow myself.*

ASPEN MATIS

Walking is a sensory escape

from the routines of daily

life, allowing us to immerse

ourselves in the present

HAPPY HEART

Regular walking leads to a happy and healthy heart in so many different ways – and the great news is that the benefits are cumulative and long-term.

Making a habit of walking improves our cardiovascular health significantly. According to the National Heart Foundation of Australia, "Walking for an average of 30 minutes or more a day can lower the risk of heart disease, stroke, and Type 2 diabetes by 30 to 40 per cent." An improvement is also seen in blood pressure levels and blood cholesterol.

In addition to its direct effects on the heart, walking also promotes overall cardiovascular fitness. It strengthens the muscles involved in respiration, improves lung function and enhances circulation – all of which contribute to better cardiovascular health. As we walk, our heart rate increases, pumping more blood throughout the body, and delivering essential oxygen and nutrients to our muscles and organs. Over time, this improves the efficiency of the cardiovascular system, making it easier for the heart to perform its job.

According to UCLA, what's more important is how fast we walk rather than for how long. We want to aim for a brisk pace, where you can still hold a conversation but feel slightly out of breath. This intensity increases the heart rate and provides a more effective cardiovascular workout.

Part Two:
WALKING FOR THE SENSES

Quite often, we walk to get to a destination. We walk with purpose, our mind on what's needed of us on arrival or cluttered by a time outside of the present – reflecting or ruminating on the past, or planning and plotting the future. Yet, parallel to all that worrying, wondering and pondering, there's a riot of natural activity taking place all around us.

Stepping into the present and engaging all of our senses makes for a completely different walk. As we tune in, everything around us seems louder, brighter, tastier, more fragrant, more tactile somehow. The colours in feathers and flora, instead of blended into the background, are unbelievably vibrant and bright.

Sounds which were muffled become clear for us to hear – the crunch of dried leaves underfoot reminding us of a time when we'd have rambunctiously kicked and played in them.

When we intentionally use our sense of smell, we're treated to freshly cut grass and heady floral scents.

If we know what to look for, we'll usually find snacks aplenty in hedgerows – from the sometimes sour taste of picked-too-early blackberries to juicy wild cherries.

As for touch, it's not something we necessarily consider when we're on a walk but it's undoubtedly there, such as the gentle tickle of a gust of wind or the cold sting of hail.

It is by tapping into our senses – smell, sound, touch, sight and even taste – that we can enjoy our surroundings in a new and wondrous way. In taking note, we become better connected with nature and ourselves. By bringing our focus to the moment, we're treated to an exquisite tapestry we could very easily have missed.

WALKING AND YOUR SENSES: SMELL

Our sense of smell is rather special because it is directly connected with the parts of the brain which regulate our emotions, known as the olfactory system. More than any of our other senses, smell evokes emotions and is most closely linked to our memories. We once relied on it for survival – it played a key role in things like foraging and hunting, connection and communication. Nowadays, it plays a crucial part in helping us to enjoy our food and is an amazing tool which can help us relieve stress, regulate our behaviour, promote healing, relaxation and comfort, and enrich our experiences.

When it comes to taking a walk, our sense of smell can enhance it in the following ways:

- With our other senses, we absorb the information, which triggers emotional reactions. Scents work the opposite way – the emotional reaction comes first and identifying the scent is secondary. This helps us to connect more deeply to our environments.

- Our sense of smell is heightened after exercise, extending the benefits beyond the walk itself and enhancing our sensory experience.

- Stimulating our sense of smell while walking synergistically boosts memory and productivity by influencing our brain activity, fostering mindfulness, and creating associations between scents and events.

- Smells become more pronounced when we consciously focus on them, enhancing awareness and deepening our connection to nature, thus promoting feelings of well-being and harmony.

I only went out for a walk,
and finally concluded to stay
out till sundown, for going out,
I found, was really going in.

JOHN MUIR

There's a wealth

of wisdom that

nature so elegantly

reveals to us

NATURE'S FRAGRANCE

Did you know that scientists have discovered that we can distinguish between one trillion scents? Whether we're walking within an urban or rural landscape, at home or away, there'll be many different aromas. Here are some we might smell as we amble:

Petrichor

When rainfall hits dry soil, it produces a calming, earthy and fresh scent called petrichor.

Ozone

After a thunderstorm, the air often carries a crisp, clean, metallic scent known as ozone, which oddly smells a little like chlorine. The smell is created when lightning splits oxygen molecules in the atmosphere, leading to the formation of ozone (O_3).

Geosmin

Within soil and freshwater environments, there are bacteria which produce a compound called geosmin. It's a pleasant earthy smell which contributes to petrichor.

Phytoncides

When walking through a forest, we're treated to scents of trees, like pine or cedar. What we can really smell are volatile organic compounds – released by plants to defend against pests and pathogens – called phytoncides. These have been shown to have a calming effect on humans, reducing our stress and anxiety.

Floral fragrance

The aromatic scents are produced by flowers to attract pollinators such as bees and butterflies. Each flower has a distinct identifiable smell. Floral smells can be emotive and remind us of particular memories.

I have walked myself into

my best thoughts.

SØREN KIERKEGAARD

A walk is a

meditation

in motion

GO ON A
"smell walk"

We've all heard the saying: "Stop and smell the roses." Going on a "smell walk" is just that – it's making a concerted effort to place our attention on the scents we notice as we walk.

Becoming absorbed in trying to sniff out the different smells around us has a meditative effect, lowering our stress levels, reducing anxiety and creating a sense of calm. It's like pressing the mute button on the hustle and bustle of our mind.

So it's time to dig out those walking shoes and get outside. It won't matter if this is a long or short walk, or whether it takes you through cityscapes, seascapes or a forest – you'll still feel the benefits if you seek out the different smells that you encounter and take a moment to actively notice and process them.

You may encounter the smell of freshly baked bread as you pass a bakery. If you're near the coast, a salty scent may waft towards you, carried on a sea breeze. The people we pass may be wearing fragrances we recognize. Not everything we smell will be pleasant, but the key is to tap into it and see if we can zoom in on what the scent evokes for us.

The next time you encounter a smell on your walk, consider the following:

- What is it?

- Can you spot where it's coming from?

- Does it evoke any memories?

- Can you sense the shift in the smell as it passes?

LOVELY LAVENDER

On our walks, we're often treated to the heady aromatics of herbs. The scent of lavender is a distinct, recognizable and evocative one. For centuries, it's been revered as a therapeutic ingredient that calms, comforts and promotes a restful night's sleep. With its delicate purple blooms and sweet herbaceous scent, lavender is a popular flower to use in aromatherapy and craft projects because the flowers retain their fragrance long after they've been dried.

If you don't have a garden, you can grow lavender in pots on your windowsill, or you could combine the benefits of walking with those of the flowers by visiting a lavender farm to harvest some. If you don't live in a lavender-growing area, plan a walk past some other aromatic crop – a wildflower meadow or other heady, scented plants could be an option – to embrace a heightened sense of smell through walking.

MAKE A LAVENDER PILLOW SPRAY

You will need:

Dried lavender

500 ml (2 cups) distilled water

1 tablespoon witch hazel

Optional: a few drops of lavender essential oil for added fragrance

Spray bottle

Method:

1. In a small saucepan, bring the distilled water to a gentle boil. Once the water is boiling, add the lavender flowers. Reduce the heat to low and simmer for 10–15 minutes. This allows the aromatic oils to infuse into the water.

2. Remove from the heat and let the lavender water cool to room temperature.

3. Once cooled, strain to remove the lavender flowers or buds and transfer to a clean spray bottle. Add 1 tablespoon of witch hazel to the spray bottle. If you'd like a stronger scent, add a few drops of lavender essential oil to enhance the fragrance of the spray.

4. Screw on the spray cap and shake gently to mix the ingredients together. Your home-made lavender pillow spray is now ready to use! Before bedtime, simply spritz a light mist of the spray onto your pillow and enjoy the sweetest of dreams.

SEE THINGS
differently

The sights we see provide our brain with an incredible amount of information about our environment. Our sense of sight helps us to perceive movement, colour, shapes, distance and textures, as well as recognizing objects, people and places. When we're out and about, sight helps us to establish our location in relation to terrain and landmarks. What's so clever about sight is that we have the ability to zoom in and focus on minute details, but can also zoom out and scan vast areas – all the while instantaneously gathering, interpreting and discerning information.

By experimenting with sight, we can follow paths we've regularly walked and see them in completely different ways.

Through a camera lens
Whether we're taking random shots or concentrating on the composition, focusing through the lens of a camera changes how we see things. We notice and absorb the information – objects, angles, light, textures, contrast patterns or movement – from a new perspective.

Through a magnifying glass

As we're merrily walking along, there's a hidden microworld that's not so apparent to the moving eye yet is in plain sight. A magnifying glass helps us to take a closer look at flowers, leaves, insects and other small objects, revealing intricate details and patterns.

Through an artist's eye

Changing the intention of the walk to one where we'll take time to sketch completely alters the view. In capturing a scene through drawing, time seems to slow down and the objects take on a new lease of life. Our interpretation by way of shapes, lines and textures unfolds as we artistically express what we can see.

LEARN THE NAMES
of the trees

Since the moment we're born, we have an inbuilt thirst for knowledge, especially in relation to what's around us. Learning about the species we see on our walks helps us to connect with nature in a new way.

Here are ten of the most commonly found trees in the world. See which ones you can spot as you amble and ramble!

Pine

There are more than 100 varieties of this evergreen tree, which are mostly found in the northern hemisphere. Astonishingly, the oldest recorded pine is almost 5,000 years old!

Oak

A haven for thousands of wildlife species, an oak is easily spotted because of its distinctive leaf shape and its acorns. Oaks symbolize strength, wisdom and power, and can reach over 30 metres (100 feet) in height.

Maple

Best known for the delicious, sweet sap that this tree produces: maple syrup! These trees are ancient too – fossil records estimate that maple trees have been around for over 60 million years.

Eucalyptus

When a eucalyptus tree is injured, it produces a sticky, rubbery substance that looks like gum, earning it the nickname "gum tree". The leaves are toxic to most animals but loved by koalas.

Birch

Thought to be one of the first trees to regenerate itself after the Ice Age, birch is a tree that's hardy and able to grow in even the poorest of soils.

Spruce

A popular choice for Christmas trees, spruce is an evergreen that has a pyramid shape and sharp, spiky needles. They can thrive in cold conditions, which has made them a symbol for hope and longevity.

Ash

A member of the olive tree family, ash is a fast-growing tree that is able to re-sprout once it has been cut down. Ash is well-used in sport, with snooker cues, oars and hockey sticks all made from its wood.

Cedar

Used a lot in the construction and woodworking industries because it's resistant to rot, cedar is quick to reproduce, easily taking over other plants in an area. Cedar produces compounds, or "phenols", which repel insects and disease.

Beech

The wood of a beech tree is very tough, with a lovely straight grain, which is why it's a solid choice in furniture making. The diameter of a beech tree's trunk can be as large as 3 metres (10 feet), making it a perfect tree to hug.

Palm

Synonymous with coconuts, palm trees also grow dates, açai and betel nuts. There are over 2,500 species of palm in the world and when planted in the right conditions, they can live for over 1,000 years.

Walking is the perfect way
of moving if you want
to see into the life of things.

ELIZABETH VON **ARNIM**

Walking is an act

of self-care,

nurturing mind,

body and soul

with each step

Don't forget to rest your legs at times, and look, *really* look

The symmetrical spots of a ladybird

The paw prints of a badger

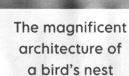

The magnificent architecture of a bird's nest

You might spot an intricate spider's web

A shy deer

LOOK AT FRACTALS
to calm and centre

You may never have heard of fractals, but you will definitely have seen them, as they're all around us. They can be spotted in mountains, coastlines, trees, river networks, vegetables, our biological structure, architecture, seashells, flowers, trees, lightning bolts and snowflakes, for example.

A fractal is a geometric pattern which infinitely recurs. What's really remarkable is that the pattern is self-repeating and self-similar, in that it repeats and appears the same no matter how zoomed-in or zoomed-out you are, or where you look on the object.

Research has shown that when we're exposed to fractals, the areas of our brain which regulate stress are activated, and stress is reduced by as much as 60 per cent. A physiological resonance occurs when we see a fractal, which relaxes, calms and soothes us. When we deliberately engage with fractals, they stimulate cognitive processes, such as pattern recognition and spatial reasoning, which can boost our creativity.

Nature has fractals in abundance, and their calming effect is almost instantaneous. The next time you're on a walk, pick up objects such as shells, fallen fern leaves and pine cones, or sit and gaze at trees swaying in the breeze, flowers waving in the wind and clouds floating in the sky, to enjoy the glories of fractal-gazing on a micro and macro scale.

EXPLORE HOW TACTILE
a walk can be

Touch quietly accompanies our walks in ways we're not always consciously aware of. Consider when you've noticed a drop or rise in temperature, or that soft, gentle breeze that's a tonic on hot and sweaty skin; the way we, almost without thinking, rub the ever-so-soft leaves of a baby maple or run our fingers through willowing and billowing blades of grass. One thing is for sure: we most definitely notice if we step on a sharp rock, when the path feels unsteady underfoot, or when we're stung by a nettle or a bee.

Touch can add an entirely different dimension to a walk. Here are some things you might try the next time you head out:

1. Run your fingers along the rough texture of tree bark

2. Feel the smoothness of polished stones or pebbles and carry one as you walk

3. Dip your hand into a cool stream or river

4. Collect different types of leaves and feel their varying textures

5. Explore the softness of moss growing on rocks or trees

6. Feel the warmth of sunlight on your skin

7. Walk barefoot on different surfaces, such as grass, sand or mud

8. Dig your toes into the sand at the beach

9. Stroke the delicate petals of flowers

10. Feel the roughness of gravel or dirt paths underfoot

11. Touch the delicate tendrils of climbing vines

12. Brush your fingers through wildflowers

13. Feel the prickly needles of pine or fir trees

14. Run your hands over the smooth surface of a wooden bridge or railing

15. Touch the rough texture of rocks or boulders along the trail

16. Play with sand or mud and sculpt it with your hands

17. Feel the coolness of shaded areas compared to sunny spots

18. Trace the intricate patterns of fern fronds

19. Explore the different textures of tree roots

20. Engage in sensory activities like balancing on fallen logs or stepping stones

*I took a walk in the woods
and came out taller than the trees.*

HENRY DAVID THOREAU

In the quiet cadence

of our steps,

we find the rhythm

of our souls

HUG A TREE

We might dismiss tree hugging as a stereotypically "hippyish" thing. In doing so, we also discount many well-documented physical and mental benefits. Research suggests that hugging trees can reduce stress, anxiety and depression, by promoting relaxation and lowering cortisol levels.

Trees emit organic compounds called phytoncides, which boost immunity and have a calming effect on humans, reducing our stress and anxiety. Additionally, when we hug a tree, we release oxytocin, the hormone associated with love, trust, bonding and a sense of calm. It's also thought that when we hug a tree, the tree helps us release negative pent-up energy, leaving us feeling supported, strong and at peace.

How to hug a tree

1. Approach a tree you feel drawn to, preferably one with a sturdy and thick trunk.

2. Lean in and embrace the tree in an all-encompassing hug, stretching your arms out as far as they'll go and leaning your cheek against the trunk.

3. Close your eyes, breathe deeply and allow yourself to just *be* – and feel held in the present moment.

TURN NATURE INTO WALL ART

When we bring nature inside our home, we bring indoors a connection with the outside world, rooting our interiors with the external landscapes and fostering tranquillity.

It turns out that making things with our hands is really good for our brain. It improves our memory and attention span, and increases a sense of well-being. There's that wonderful feeling of pride, too, which lives on long after the craft has ended.

You will need:

A photo or box frame

Paper

Natural materials

Gather your materials

While you're walking outdoors, peruse the path for anything which catches your interest – be that a fallen acorn, a distinctive leaf, a piece of fallen tree bark which has a tactile texture, a rock that is an unusual colour or shape, fallen dried flowers or pine cones. Anything which sparks joy or curiosity. With an attitude of reverence, pick up any items you're drawn to, being careful not to disturb living wildlife.

Pull it all together

Find a flat surface outdoors or indoors where you can comfortably arrange your materials. Lay out your paper and place the treasures on top, arranging them in various positions to create visually appealing compositions. Consider the shapes, the patterns and tones. Keep tweaking until you have a piece of art you're proud to hang in your home. Glue your items onto the paper and display them in your frame.

GO BAREFOOT

For most of human history, we went about our days barefoot. It's only in more recent times that people in many parts of the world have taken to wearing shoes. Not only do shoes alter the way we'd more naturally use our feet and ankles, but they also act as a barrier to something called grounding or earthing.

Research indicates that connecting our skin directly with the earth or water can alleviate stress, anxiety and depression by increasing relaxation and reducing cortisol levels. When we're barefoot outside, we absorb free ions from the earth's natural energy, which have been shown to enhance immunity and impart a sense of calm. This is grounding or earthing.

To engage in grounding, find a spot where you feel drawn, preferably with lush grass or soft soil beneath your feet. Stand barefoot on the earth, allowing its energy to flow through you. Close your eyes, take deep breaths and simply be present in the moment, embracing the natural connection between yourself and the earth. You'll invigorate your body, clear your mind and nourish your soul.

Grounding or earthing also:

- Improves mood
- Boosts energy levels
- Reduces mental stress
- Improves quality of sleep
- Reduces inflammation

- Reduces chronic pain
- Relieves headaches
- Relieves muscle tension
- Improves blood pressure
- Speeds up healing and recovery

LISTEN OUT

Wherever and whenever we go for a stroll, we're enveloped in a symphony of sound, which can have a profound effect on how we feel. Those sounds will vary dramatically, depending on where we take our walk.

A stroll in a busy city might be accompanied by the barking of a dog, the laughter of a group as they huddle together on the pavement and the honking of a car horn. A humdrum we might find soothing and comforting, as it makes us feel part of a vibrant community.

Rural walks have their own soundtrack, with birds cheeping merrily away, the steady flow of water as it crashes and careens on rocks, and the trees groaning as they sway in the wind.

Wherever we walk, there'll be the sounds we make, which contribute to the soundtrack: thumping footsteps, grit scraping underfoot, the squelching of mud as we navigate a muddy patch, the crunching of leaves as we place one foot in front of the other, the way our breath changes depending on an ascent or descent, and the heady "ooh" and "ahh" after we've traversed a particularly steep and challenging hill.

Filtering sounds and trying to identify them can anchor us into the present moment, heightening our awareness and appreciation of our surroundings. Whether urban or rural, the sounds of our walk provide a unique soundscape to our journey, connecting us to the rhythm and pulse of life all around us.

TELL STORIES
WITH SOUND

When we're taking a walk, it can feel as though there aren't many distinct sounds or as though they're all muffled together. As we relax, we'll be surprised by the sheer variety of sounds we can tune into.

As you listen carefully, notice that the sounds evoke different emotions, thoughts or ideas within you. Perhaps there's a distant bird call that sounds full of longing, which acts as a starting point for a heart-warming love story. The rushing of a nearby river might call to mind an epic adventure. The beeping of a distant car horn could inspire a tale about a flying vehicle.

Take one of the sounds you've identified and play with it. Don't be afraid to go off on the wildest of tangents as you allow your imagination to run away with itself, crafting stories, limericks, songs or characters as you walk, using sound as your inspiration, your muse.

LEARN THE 5-4-3-2-1 METHOD FOR ANXIETY RELIEF

Walking, in and of itself, helps to prevent and lessen the symptoms of anxiety. For those times which are particularly overwhelming and distressing, the 5-4-3-2-1 technique can effectively bring us back to our senses, isolating each one in turn. This calms our fight-or-flight response, helping us to tap into the awareness of our surroundings. Focusing on experiencing the present moment in all its sensory detail can help to slow a racing mind, alleviating those feelings of worry and panic, and bringing about a much-needed sense of calm.

How to use the 5-4-3-2-1 technique on your walk

Look around you and notice:

- **5** things you can see
- **4** things you can feel
- **3** things you can hear
- **2** things you can smell
- **1** thing you can taste

GO ON A SCAVENGER HUNT FOR SOUNDS

A scavenger hunt for sounds is a really fun way to sharpen listening skills and experience a walk as you've never done before.

As you walk, listen out carefully for the following sounds, and cross them off when you hear them:

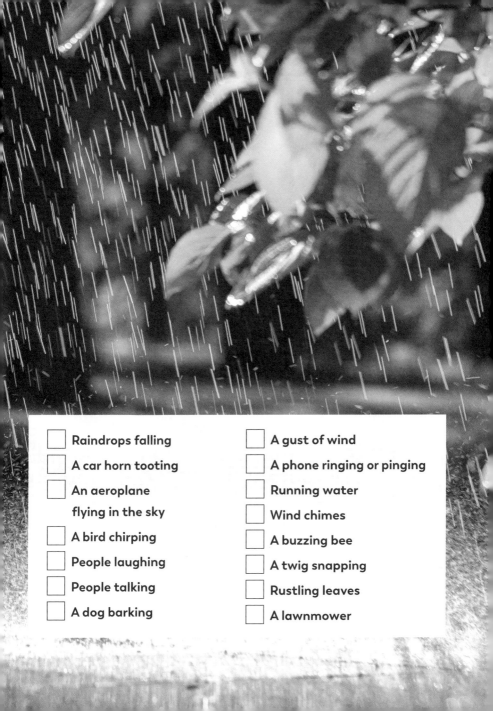

- [ ] Raindrops falling
- [ ] A car horn tooting
- [ ] An aeroplane flying in the sky
- [ ] A bird chirping
- [ ] People laughing
- [ ] People talking
- [ ] A dog barking
- [ ] A gust of wind
- [ ] A phone ringing or pinging
- [ ] Running water
- [ ] Wind chimes
- [ ] A buzzing bee
- [ ] A twig snapping
- [ ] Rustling leaves
- [ ] A lawnmower

WALKS WITH TASTE

Walking is synonymous with food, isn't it? Rambling about doesn't half work up an appetite and, wherever we happen to be, there's usually plenty to whet it too. If we've come prepared, there's a snack or two in our backpack – perhaps even a picnic and a refreshing drink. If we haven't, fret not, because the hedgerows, parks and streets often have an abundance of food available. Foraging, snack vans, cafés and markets can provide the goods.

Eating outdoors always feels special. Eating al fresco heightens our sense of taste, which increases the deliciousness of savoury and sweet delights.

There's often an adventure, escapade or mishap moment when we invite nature to join us as we dine. A foreboding cloud which threatens to pour on us, the seagulls milling and mincing about, an ant invasion, an accidental spill... It just adds to the memories and fun of it all.

TUCK INTO
nature's pantry

Turning to the land for sustenance is something we've done since the beginning of human existence. Foraging is the act of searching for and gathering wild food resources from nature. It involves identifying, harvesting and, sometimes, processing edible plants, fruits, nuts, seeds, mushrooms and other natural materials found in the wild.

Foragers rely on their knowledge of local flora and fauna to identify edible species and distinguish them from toxic or inedible ones. They often use a combination of observation, experience, field guides and expert guidance to ensure the safety of their foraging activities. Importantly, foragers are mindful of local, ethical and environmental considerations, such as sustainability and conservation, and private property rights.

Caution! Never ingest anything you haven't identified as 100 per cent safe to eat – many plants, as well as fungi and berries, are highly toxic and fatal if consumed, and many safe wild foods have poisonous lookalikes, so should be avoided. Stick to well-known plants and avoid anything that may have been sprayed. Once you know what you're doing, however, what can be more rewarding than going out for a walk and finding an array of fresh, nutritious food – foraged and free – and then sitting down to enjoy it?

COMMON WILD EDIBLES
FOUND IN NATURE'S PANTRY

Berries
Such as blackberries, raspberries, blueberries and strawberries, which are not only delicious but also packed with vitamins and antioxidants.

Nuts and seeds
Including walnuts, chestnuts, acorns and sunflower seeds, which provide essential fats, protein and energy.

Wild greens
Like dandelion greens, nettles and chickweed, which are nutritious and versatile additions to salads, soups and stir-fries.

Herbs and spices
Such as wild garlic, wild thyme and elderflower, which add aromatic flavour to dishes.

Mushrooms
Including chanterelles, morels and porcini, which offer earthy, umami-rich tastes and textures.

All truly great thoughts are conceived by walking.

FRIEDRICH NIETZSCHE

Walking isn't just about

getting from A to B —

it's about the experiences

and the discoveries we

make along the way

SCRUMPTIOUS WILD BLACKBERRY CRUMBLE

Towards the end of summer, hedgerows are full to the brim with ripe, juicy, irresistible blackberries. Take a container on your walk to carry your bounty – picking enough to allow for the handfuls that you'll undoubtedly eat before you make it home. Once in the kitchen, wash the blackberries and then make this crowd-pleasing and rustic dessert with your foraged goods.

You will need:

500 g (17 ½ oz) fresh blackberries

100 g (3 ½ oz) granulated sugar

1 tablespoon lemon juice

100 g (3 ½ oz) plain flour

75 g (2 ½ oz) rolled oats

75 g (2 ½ oz) brown sugar

75 g (2 ½ oz) unsalted butter, chilled and diced

Pinch of salt

Vanilla ice cream, custard or whipped cream, to serve (optional)

Method:

1. Preheat your oven to 180°C (350°F). Grease a baking dish or individual ramekins with butter or cooking spray.

2. In a mixing bowl, gently toss the blackberries with the granulated sugar and lemon juice until evenly coated. Transfer the blackberries to the prepared baking dish or ramekins, spreading them out evenly.

3. In a separate bowl, combine the flour, rolled oats, brown sugar and a pinch of salt. Add the chilled diced butter to the dry ingredients and use your fingers or a pastry cutter to rub the butter into the flour mixture until it resembles coarse breadcrumbs.

4. Sprinkle the crumble mixture evenly over the blackberries in the baking dish or ramekins, covering them completely.

5. Place the baking dish or ramekins on a baking tray and bake in the preheated oven for 30–35 minutes, or until the crumble topping is golden brown and the blackberries are bubbling.

6. Remove from the oven and allow to cool slightly before serving.

7. Serve the blackberry crumble warm, topped with a scoop of vanilla ice cream, a splash of custard or a dollop of whipped cream if desired.

NATURE
as medicine

There's something gratifying in making tea from leaves we've foraged. Not only does it help us to feel more connected with nature, which in itself boosts our sense of well-being, but it also helps us to start looking at our surroundings a little bit differently. Instead of passing plants by, we begin to notice ingredients and materials.

Nettles grow rampantly in nature – they're here, there and everywhere. We're used to avoiding them because they have a horrible itchy sting which can cause a nasty rash. Despite that, nettle tea can soothe hay fever symptoms. In fact, it's a remedy that's been used for centuries!

Rich in antioxidants, nettle tea also helps to reduce inflammation and ease joint pain, as well as providing a rich source of iron and boosting our immune system. Not a fan of nettle tea? There are many other plants you can make tea from. Try rosehip, bilberry, dandelion or camomile instead.

How to make nettle tea

1. We all know how a brush with nettles can sting for hours, so we're going to want to don a pair of gloves to protect our hands. The best nettles are those in a wild setting, as that limits the effect of pesticides and pollution.

2. Next up is harvesting. It's the top few inches of the plant we're after, where the leaves are young and tender. You can pinch these leaves out or use scissors to snip them.

3. Once home, rinse the leaves under cold water to remove any dirt or bugs. Place a handful of leaves in a teapot and fill it with boiling water.

4. After 10–15 minutes, the leaves will have released all of the beneficial compounds into the water. Strain the tea through a fine mesh and pour into a mug.

5. Enjoy!

Nettle tea is safe to drink daily, as long as you're not pregnant or breastfeeding.

Part Three:
WALKING FOR MENTAL AND SPIRITUAL WELL-BEING

Life can sometimes wear us out and weigh us down, taking a toll on how we feel about ourselves. When the mental, emotional and physical burdens become too heavy to carry, we can find ourselves struggling to keep on keeping on. Everyone feels this way from time to time but sometimes it's for a prolonged period, and we start to experience prevalent low mood and symptoms of depression and anxiety, which can feel scary and unsettling.

We all deserve a life that lights us up: one where we look ahead and feel excited about what's to come; a life that's not just full of trouble and strife, but that has lots of moments of reprieve and many jots of joy.

Day-to-day, it's all too easy to get caught up in the hullabaloo. We think that by giving more and doing more, we'll get more and be more. On the contrary, it's in the moments we step away from it all that the magic occurs: the healing, emoting, solution-finding and self-care.

That's what walking gives us, and so much more. Whether it's a brisk or gentle walk, for ten minutes or three hours, in the wilderness or through city streets, we get the chance to tune out of the humdrum and tune inward. Walking allows us to connect deeply with our thoughts and feelings. Each step provides an opportunity to reflect, process emotions and gain new perspectives, which can alleviate anxiety and lift our mood.

On a spiritual level, walking can be a meditative practice that grounds us and brings a sense of peace. As we move through our surroundings, we become more mindful of our interconnectedness to the world around us and its beauty. This mindfulness enhances our overall sense of spiritual well-being.

A seemingly ordinary walk can lead us to extraordinary places within ourselves.

THE STEPS OF SELF-CARE

Walking is a gentle yet powerfully holistic act of self-care which nurtures our well-being on every level: physically, emotionally, mentally and spiritually. It really is as simple as putting one foot in front of the other as we follow a beaten or unbeaten track.

When life gets on top of us and we find our mental health spiralling downward, taking a walk is an accessible act of self-care which can foster a sense of accomplishment, as well as cultivating a sense of balance and strength. The interconnectedness with nature helps us to feel rooted and grounded within ourselves and the world at large.

As we walk, we get the chance to press pause on the world around us and take a respite from the chaos, expectations and burdens of daily life. The movement of our body helps to dissipate tension, stress and worry. The rhythm of those movements helps to still the chatter in our mind, affording us much-needed quietude.

MEDITATE ON THE MOVE

Life can be all hustle and bustle. Finding moments when our mind can "rest" is more important now than ever before. A mindful walk is meditation in motion – it's a way to feel grounded and calm. Since the focus is on walking itself, this is a mindfulness practice that can be done anywhere.

You can start with a walk as short as ten minutes and build up. During any meditation, it's normal for the mind to wander. When we keep bringing our mind back to the present moment, we strengthen our meditation muscles; much of the work is in the "noticing". The more we practise mindfulness, the more easily we can access it throughout the day.

How to do a meditative walk

1. Begin your walk, taking care to remove any distractions. As you take each step, focus your attention on the sensations you feel – the movement of your feet, the roll of your hips, the way your body shifts and moves, and the contact with the ground beneath you.

2. Settle into a confident yet steady pace, tuning into the rhythm of your body moving.

3. When your mind wanders, gently bring it back to the present moment – to your senses and sensations.

4. Be kind and gentle with yourself as you keep returning to the awareness of how it feels to be walking.

5. Notice how much calmer you feel once you have finished your walk.

Walking is a simple but powerful way to boost your mood and improve your overall health.

MICHELLE OBAMA

Walking provides the

chance to connect with

our deepest desires

and our wildest

aspirations

BE AN EARLY BIRD

We all have a circadian rhythm, which is a natural, internal process that regulates our sleep-wake cycle and repeats roughly every 24 hours. This internal "clock" plays a pivotal role in determining when we feel awake and alert versus when we feel sleepy and ready for bed. Additionally, it helps to synchronize our bodily functions with the time of day, and things like hormone production, body temperature and metabolism.

Environmental factors – such as whether it's light or dark, the temperature, the foods and drinks we consume, medication, stress, noise and artificial light – influence our circadian rhythm. Some of these factors will be a supportive influence and others can make it go off-kilter, leading to disrupted sleep, change in behaviour, and mood disorders like depression and anxiety.

Walking outdoors aligns with our natural circadian rhythm, particularly if we take a stroll in the morning, when we're most sensitive to light. It also exposes us to varying levels of natural light, which influences the production of melatonin, the hormone that regulates sleep. Morning walks can help to kick-start our internal clock, signalling to our bodies that it's time to wake up and be alert, while evening walks can promote relaxation and prepare us for a restful sleep.

RUB THOSE
WORRIES AWAY

For centuries, people have been using smooth oval-shaped stones with a dipped curve "thumb indent" (think ever-so-slight bowl shape) to help ease their worries. They do so by rubbing the stone between their finger and thumb or by fidgeting with it when they feel overwhelmed. Much in the same way we'd use a fidget toy, these worry stones offer a simple yet effective way to soothe us and are a great stimming tool.

Often made from crystals or gemstones, anything that's of a similar shape or size counts, as long as it has a smooth and tactile surface. Traditionally, these stones have been worn smooth by bodies of water, so look for them as you walk along the shoreline of a beach or scattered along a riverbank. Choose a stone which fits comfortably in the palm of your hand, and that feels pleasing to touch and toy with.

Having a worry stone can improve focus, aid feelings of security, and ease anxiety and worry, as well as bringing a sense of comfort and calm. Next time you're out walking, keep an eye out for the perfect stone. Carry it with you to augment the calming effect of your walk.

BREATHE IN, BREATHE OUT

Purposefully paying attention to our breath while walking is also known as a breathwalk. Taking a breathwalk is about savouring the simple joys of life, embracing the journey as it unfolds, and being fully present in the here and now. Similar to practising yoga, incorporating various breathing techniques into a mindful walking practice can enhance its benefits and deepen our connection with our breath and body.

Here are a few techniques you could try:

One breath, one step

With each inhalation, take a single step forward, focusing on the sensation of your foot connecting with the ground beneath you. With each exhalation, take another step, allowing your breath to guide your movement with grace and intention.

Simple and steady

Begin by simply noticing your breath as you walk. Pay attention to its rhythm, the sensation of air entering and leaving your body, and the rise and fall of your chest and abdomen. Allow your breath to anchor you in the present moment as you move forward with each step.

Breath of fire

Please note: if you have hypertension, are pregnant, or suffer from vertigo, heart disease or seizures, you should not practise this breathing technique.

Breathe rapidly and rhythmically through your nostrils as you walk. Focus on forceful exhales, letting the inhales happen naturally. Maintain a steady pace and intensity, staying mindful of how the rapid breath affects your body and mind.

TREAT YOURSELF TO A SELF-KINDNESS WALK

Our internal chatter isn't always the kindest. In fact, it can sometimes be downright cruel. We'd certainly never talk to another person in that way. Furthermore, we definitely wouldn't expect them to thrive under such conditions.

The way we speak to ourselves matters and it's incredibly impactful. Our thoughts are the basis of our behaviours and the actions we take. If we're constantly putting ourselves down, we're unlikely to feel equipped to put ourselves out there. Living with a constant stream of negative internal noise will not serve us well: it'll leave us feeling despondent, helpless and low.

These things are habits that are formed over time, which means we can replace them with a new one: self-kindness. To begin with, it feels awkward to be kind to ourselves, but that's simply because we're out of practice. Don't let that deter you – keep at it, and with time it'll start to feel as though it's coming more naturally.

One way we can treat ourselves is to go on a regular self-kindness walk. The rules are nice and simple but the difference it can make is huge.

Pack a favourite snack, choose a route you enjoy, bring along a much-loved book and, for the entire walk, remind yourself of:

- All of the times you were kind to others
- Things you are proud of
- Your accomplishments
- Memories that make you feel happy
- The lyrics of songs that uplift you

GET A CREATIVITY BOOST

If you find yourself in the middle of writer's block or feeling as though your creativity has dried up, the solution is staring at you from the window: go for a walk. It really is as simple as that. Charles Darwin, Steve Jobs, Nikola Tesla, Ludwig van Beethoven, Marie Curie and far too many more to mention have extolled the virtues of walking in helping them to create life-changing solutions, products and art.

Their claims are backed by science too. A study by Stanford University found that a walk can improve creative ideation by as much as 60 per cent. Interestingly it's the physical act of walking

not the environment within which you're walking, that does all of the magic. It's thought that the break from executive functioning allows our mind to relax, change perspective, wander and play. Even when we sit back down after the walk, the study found, our creative juices continue to flow.

So next time you feel at your wit's end because the creativity just isn't flowing, take that walk!

ORNAMENTAL
sticks

Look closely and you'll notice that there's treasure to be found underfoot. Fallen branches, driftwood and twigs are not just fallen branches, driftwood and twigs. Nuh-hu, they're blank canvases ripe and ready for us to unleash our creativity.

There is no such thing as the "perfect" natural canvas. They come in all shapes, sizes and textures. You'll know the right one when you see it – it'll be the one (or more) that catches your eye as you scan the forest floor, park or beach – on a woodland, town or coastal walk.

Painting sticks is one of those meditative and therapeutic activities for people of all ages and artistic talent – especially if we don't overthink it and go with the painting flow. We can freehand, use painter's tape to section areas off, draw with paint pens or paint with brushes and acrylics. There really is no right or wrong way to decorate sticks but if you're really struggling with inspiration, head over to Pinterest and search for "painted sticks".

Next time you're out and about, keeping an eye out for fallen sticks to decorate and display at home can add a touch of interest and inspiration, transforming your walk into a treasure hunt – and forever providing a keepsake of that particular walk on that particular day.

ON OVERCOMING
obstacles

We weren't born knowing how to walk. Just think about those first wobbly steps we took as toddlers, tentatively venturing forward, arms outstretched for balance, uncertain what we were doing. Yet, with each stumble and fall, bruise and graze, we picked ourselves up and tried again. Gradually, we gained confidence and became fantastic walkers. So much so that it's autopilot to us now.

Similarly, when things don't go to plan, we can draw on how we approached learning to walk. We didn't beat ourselves up for "failing" when we fell; we turned those missteps into valuable information on what not to do next time. We learned from what worked and from what didn't.

Walking is a great metaphor for overcoming obstacles and building confidence. Each time we navigated uneven terrain, tackled steep inclines, pushed through fatigue or got lost and had to find our way, we confronted fears, drew on determination and resilience, and unwittingly grew in confidence.

EXPERIMENT WITH
natural dyes

Did you know that you can create the most stunning fabric dye from things commonly found on walks? It's a method that's centuries-old but has had somewhat of a resurgence because it's a sustainable and environmentally friendly way to create beautiful, one-of-a-kind textiles.

This is far from an exhaustive list – and part of the fun is in experimenting. However, you can dye fabrics with:

- Lichens (e.g. usnea, evernia, parmelia)
- Cones (e.g. alder cones, pine cones)
- Leaves (e.g. maple, oak, birch, indigo, henna, sorrel)
- Flower petals (e.g. marigold, dandelion, rose, hibiscus, camomile)
- Berries (e.g. blackberries, elderberries, blueberries, mulberries, sloe)
- Tree bark (e.g. oak, willow, eucalyptus)
- Roots (e.g. madder, turmeric)
- Nuts and seeds (e.g. annatto seeds, acorns, pecans, walnut shells)
- Vegetable scraps (e.g. onion skins, beet tops)
- Fungi (e.g. mushrooms)
- Herbs (e.g. camomile, sage, lavender, rosemary, bay leaves, thyme)
- Spices (e.g. cinnamon, paprika, turmeric, saffron)
- Seaweed

The results and depth of colour will vary depending on the amount of materials you've collected, the type of fabric, how the fabric is prepared and how long it is bathed in the dye. You can enjoy hunting for some of these items on your next walk!

The rhythm of walking generates a kind of rhythm of thinking, and the passage through a landscape echoes or stimulates the passage through a series of thoughts.

REBECCA SOLNIT

Walking is

natural therapy,

unburdening

the heart and mind

Nature is generous with
its gifts of beauty

Perfect perches
for swings

Magnificent
meadows

Wondrous
waterfalls

Breathtaking sunsets

Stunning rainbows

CONNECT WITH YOUR INNER CHILD

Watch a child on a walk and you'll see a small person who is brimming with energy, spontaneity and creativity. Rather than walk in a straight line, they weave in and out, climb up and over, and find the littlest of things awe-inspiring.

As we age, it's all too easy to lose touch with that sense of wonder and playfulness. Life is busy and, as a result, we find ourselves caught up in the humdrum from morning to night, rarely seeking out space to live a little.

Yet, within each of us lies an inner child yearning to be rediscovered – the part of ourselves that finds joy in the simplest of objects and still sees magic in the mundane. Whether it's the fresh air, muscle memory or the influence of nature, when we're outdoors on a walk, some of the constraints of adulthood feel removed. Our inner child emerges more readily, eager to explore, discover and play. We easily remember what it's like to see our surroundings through younger eyes.

In a world that often feels hectic and overwhelming, tapping into our inner child during walks offers a much-needed breather. It reminds us that life is meant to be lived with curiosity, imagination and laughter. So, the next time you find yourself outdoors, take a cue from the children around you and let your inner child lead the way.

IT'S NOT JUST
child's play

If it's been a long while since we've let loose our inner child, they might need some encouragement to join the fun. Taking inspiration from a carefree child on a walk, here are some activities you can try on your walk, to unearth that innate playfulness.

Grass whistle

Pluck a thick blade of grass and position it between your thumbs so it's taut, and then blow to produce a whistle sound.

Pooh sticks

The next time you're on a walk and you come across a bridge over running water, play Pooh sticks. Each player selects a stick, drops it into the water at the same time, and then eagerly runs to the downstream side of the bridge to see whose stick emerges first, declaring the winner.

Dandelion wishes

Pick a dandelion puff – a dandelion that's no longer yellow and has gone to seed. Blow on the seeds and make a wish. Let the wind carry your dreams and wishes away to eventually come true (so they say!).

Sycamore helicopter

Pick a fallen sycamore seed and make sure it's a proper pairing that looks like a set of helicopter wings. Stand tall, release and watch the "helicopter" land on the ground. Also try field maple seeds, ash seeds and Norway maple seeds.

Daisy chain

Gather a handful of daisies and, with your thumbnail, carve a slit in the stem of the first one. Take your second daisy and weave its stem through the slit on the first daisy. Once you've pulled the stem through, make a slit in the stem of the second daisy and weave the third daisy's stem through it. Repeat until you have a long enough chain to make into a necklace, bracelet or crown. You'll need to link the last daisy to the first. Do that by making a slit in the stem of the last daisy and then carefully pushing the head of the first daisy through.

Puddles

You'll need wellies. Once equipped, just jump and splash in puddles to your heart's content!

Skimming stones

There is an art and a science to this, but practice makes perfect. Take a waterside walk and comb the shores of the pond, lake, river or sea to find some smooth, flat stones which you can easily hold in your hand. Apparently, you need to throw the stone at a (very precise) angle of 20°. But, honestly, just try, try and try again. Have fun with it – a simple way to add an element of entertainment to any walk along the waterside.

WALK
and talk

Whether it's a leisurely stroll through the park or a brisk walk along a scenic trail, the simple act of walking with our friends or loved ones holds immeasurable value. It's a wonderful way to nurture our relationships, and to connect, catch up and have fun. The shared experience creates lasting memories and strengthens bonds.

Holding hands, linking arms or simply walking side by side releases oxytocin – the "love", "connectedness" or "cuddle" hormone – which promotes feelings of trust, intimacy, mutual respect and positive regard. This in turn releases serotonin, the "happy" hormone, helping us to feel content and optimistic. It also has a brilliant effect on heart health, lowering blood pressure and reducing stress and anxiety.

After a while, we'll find ourselves walking in harmony "as one", our steps completely in sync. This synchronization of movement is a non-verbal form of social communication that brings with it a deep feeling of unity and solidarity, and can have a meditative effect.

We'll find that as conversation flows, it's sometimes easier to open up and share our vulnerability with people who are beside us rather than opposite us. The social and emotional aspects of this mean that we might share our problems, support one another through challenging times, provide words of encouragement, and enjoy bouts of laughter as we joke and jest.

A walk in nature walks

the soul back home.

MARY DAVIS

When walking together,

we not only get to enjoy

the benefits of walking –

we magnify them

and grow closer

WALK TO
work it out

Walking has long been recognized as a powerful tool for working through conflict or finding solutions to challenging problems. When tensions are high or our mind feels cluttered with hurt feelings, taking a walk can bring clarity, perspective and solutions you mightn't ordinarily have come up with had you tried to resolve the issue while seated face to face.

In moments of conflict with others, walking provides a physical outlet for releasing pent-up emotions and reducing stress levels. Stepping away from the intensity of the situation allows us to cool off emotionally and approach the issue with a calmer, more rational mindset. As we walk, the rhythmic movement can help to regulate our breathing and calm our nervous system, making it easier to communicate effectively and find common ground.

Walking side by side creates a non-confrontational environment, eliminating the pressure of face-to-face interaction. The physical act of walking can symbolize moving forward together in alignment, toward resolution and understanding.

Moreover, the change of scenery that walking provides can stimulate creativity and problem-solving. Walking together offers an opportunity to bridge divides, build trust and strengthen relationships.

Walking can also be a powerful natural therapy to work through sadness, grief or other difficult emotions in a calm outdoor environment, releasing physical and emotional tension with each step.

FIND YOUR

people

Walking can be a fantastic social activity. Going on a walk with others expands the mental, physical and emotional benefits of walking. When we connect with others in this way, we reduce loneliness and isolation by feeling part of a community of people who share a common interest – that's powerful. We might make new friends, feel more supported and enjoy a renewed motivation to walk more.

It's highly likely that there's already a walking group in your area. Quite often, these have Facebook pages and/or web pages which give a sense of what they might be like to join. However, if you can't find a local group, why not start your own?

Plan it all out

Consider where and when you'll meet. It's useful to create some guidelines on things like behaviour, communication, safety and inclusivity. Lastly, you'll want to have some walks under your belt offering differing distances, difficulty levels, destinations and themes.

Recruit members

Reach out to friends, family, neighbours and community members who may be interested in joining your walking group. Use social media, flyers and word of mouth to spread the word.

Nurture connections

Provide ample opportunity for people to get to know one another. Have a "buddy" system where new members are paired with a more experienced one. You may have quick-fire icebreaker questions to answer as you're walking. Ensure you provide pit stops to encourage natural breaks to gather and chat.

FUEL UP WITH HOME-MADE TRAIL MIX

A convenient, healthy and wholesome snack to tuck into whether you're hiking, strolling or simply in need of a snack while on the go. Packed with protein, fibre and heart-healthy fats, this home-made trail mix will keep you energized and fuelled.

You will need:

100 g (3 ½ oz) almonds

100 g (3 ½ oz) cashews

100 g (3 ½ oz) pumpkin seeds

100 g (3 ½ oz) dried cranberries

100 g (3 ½ oz) dried apricots, chopped

50 g (1 ¾ oz) dark chocolate chips or chunks

Method:

1. Preheat the oven to 150°C (300°F) and line a baking tray with parchment paper.

2. Spread the almonds, cashews and pumpkin seeds evenly onto the prepared baking tray.

3. Roast the nuts and seeds in the preheated oven for 10–12 minutes, or until lightly golden and fragrant. Keep a close eye on them to prevent burning.

4. Once roasted, remove the nuts and seeds from the oven and allow them to cool completely.

5. In a large mixing bowl, combine the roasted nuts and seeds with the dried cranberries, chopped dried apricots and dark chocolate chips.

6. Gently toss the ingredients together until evenly distributed.

7. Transfer the trail mix to an airtight container, or resealable and reusable bags, for storage.

FIVE WALK-INSPIRED WRITING PROMPTS

Writing is such a powerful way to process what you go through, and it has been shown to reduce stress, anxiety and depression. Not only does it provide the space for reflection and expression, but it also helps us to acknowledge and accept thoughts and feelings. Many solutions have been brought about by the act of putting pen to paper. There's a palpable lightening of the mental load when we pour our mind onto the page.

The best bit about writing is that it's portable. We can take our notebooks and pens on a walk and once we've found a peaceful and comfortable spot – perhaps overlooking a river or tucked away within a copse of trees – we can let the words flow.

While freewriting is beneficial, it can feel like a daunting place to begin if it's not a habit you're accustomed to. To start with, you might find it helpful to have some writing prompts. Here are some to get you going:

The path less travelled
Write about a character who decides to take a different route on their daily walk and discovers something unexpected along the way.

The wanderer's journal
Imagine finding an old journal filled with entries from someone's walks. Write about the stories, musings or secrets revealed within its pages.

A walk through time
Take a walk through a historic neighbourhood and imagine the lives of the people who once walked those same streets. Write a short story or poem inspired by your observations.

The hidden path
Create a story about a character who discovers a hidden pathway in the woods during their walk. What mysteries or adventures await them?

The meeting place
Write a scene where two characters unexpectedly cross paths during their walks and strike up a conversation that changes both of their lives.

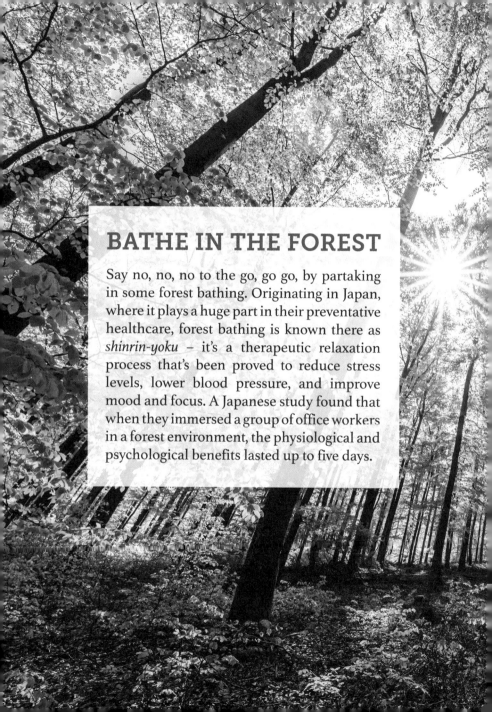

BATHE IN THE FOREST

Say no, no, no to the go, go go, by partaking in some forest bathing. Originating in Japan, where it plays a huge part in their preventative healthcare, forest bathing is known there as *shinrin-yoku* – it's a therapeutic relaxation process that's been proved to reduce stress levels, lower blood pressure, and improve mood and focus. A Japanese study found that when they immersed a group of office workers in a forest environment, the physiological and psychological benefits lasted up to five days.

Try it

The recommended length of a therapeutic forest-bathing session is two hours. That said, you'll still feel benefits on shorter walks. The key is to:

- Silence your phone notifications
- Walk slowly and mindfully
- Absorb and observe nature – the scents, the scenes, the sounds, the peace, the calm
- Focus on your senses, isolating them so you experience the walk through one sense at a time
- Tap into your body – feel your breath as you inhale and exhale, and notice your heart beating

Allow yourself to feel grounded in the present moment.

TAKE A REFRESHING DIP

Where it's safe and appropriate to do so, combining wild swimming with a walk has a synergistic effect which amplifies the benefits of both activities. Not only does it provide a refreshing splash of cold water after working up a sweat, but it also enhances the overall enjoyment of your outdoor adventure. Here's how:

It's a full-body workout

Swimming engages multiple muscle groups, providing a low-impact cardiovascular workout that promotes strength, flexibility and endurance.

So refreshing and invigorating

Immersing yourself in natural water after a walk can be incredibly refreshing, rejuvenating and invigorating, revitalizing your body and mind.

A natural stress-relief

Wild swimming in natural bodies of water offers a unique form of stress relief, as the tranquil environment and soothing water help to calm the mind, reduce anxiety and promote relaxation.

Cold-water therapy

Exposure to cold water is being studied for its reported mental health benefits, providing relief to some people suffering from anxious or depressive thoughts and feelings. However, be aware that there are safety implications, particularly for people with existing medical conditions. To avoid cold water shock, ensure you enter the water slowly and allow your body time to get used to the temperature.

Improves mood

The release of endorphins during physical activity, such as swimming and walking, promotes feelings of happiness and well-being, uplifting your mood and outlook on life.

Enhances circulation and recovery

Swimming improves blood circulation and aids in muscle recovery after a walk, providing gentle resistance to alleviate soreness and tension.

Provides a sense of adventure

Incorporating wild swimming into your walk adds an element of adventure – allowing you to discover new swimming spots along your route – and makes your outdoor experiences more exciting and memorable.

LOOK UP AT THE STARS

We're usually snuggling up and preparing to turn in when it's dark outside, but we're missing out on pure magic. Being outdoors when it's dark opens up a whole new world where everything looks and feels different. Night-time can be an incredibly peaceful time to go for a walk, and a night hike under a full moon is especially memorable. Our senses are heightened and our perception of space, distance, and life itself, is altered. Under the star-studded skies and the soft glow of moonlight, the ordinary feels extraordinary.

On a clear night, you'll see stars aplenty. Look more closely and you'll be able to pinpoint constellations and even moving satellites. In order to spot constellations, we connect the dots (the stars) to depict objects, animals or a person – a bit like playing dot to dot.

How to spot Orion

One of the easiest and perhaps best-known constellations is Orion, which is named after a hunter in Greek mythology. It's a human-form figure in the sky and can be seen from all around the world.

More than a dozen stars make up Orion. First, we need to locate Orion's Belt. This is three supergiant stars which appear close together, evenly spaced in a line: the "waist" of the hunter.

Keeping Orion's Belt in sight, you should be able to make out an hourglass shape. The two bright stars above the belt are his shoulders and fill out his upper body. If you follow the brightest star above his belt to the east, travelling along his arm, you should be able to spot his "bow".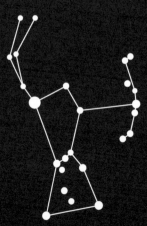

The two bright stars below his belt are his feet. Within that space below his belt, hanging from it, you may be able to make out his sword.

The world reveals itself to those who travel on foot.

WERNER HERZOG

As we walk, we cultivate

mindfulness: observing

and acknowledging our

emotions without judgement

NATURE sketching

Nature sketching is an art form that connects us to the world around us and is a perfect companion to walking. It allows us to observe and capture the beauty of plants, animals and landscapes. We can play with composition, abstract art, realism and creating freely, with no constraints or self-judgement.

Choose your tools

Start by gathering the materials you'll need. Opt for a sketchbook with heavyweight paper to withstand the wind. Bring along a range of pencils (such as HB, 2B and 4B) for varying line weights, as well as erasers, sharpeners and a portable sketching stool or cushion for comfort.

Find inspiration

Head outdoors to a setting that inspires you, whether it's a serene woodland, a tranquil meadow or a rugged coastline. Take your time to observe the plants, animals and landscapes around you, paying attention to their shapes, textures and patterns. Look for interesting compositions and focal points that catch your eye.

Start sketching

Begin by lightly sketching the basic shapes and outlines of your subject using a light pencil. Focus on capturing the overall form and proportions before adding finer details. Use quick, gestural lines to convey movement and energy, and don't worry about

making mistakes – nature sketching is about capturing the essence of your subject rather than aiming for perfection.

Add detail and texture

Once you're happy with the overall composition, start adding details and textures to your sketch. Use different pencil grades to create depth and contrast, experimenting with shading techniques such as hatching, cross-hatching and stippling to render textures like bark, leaves and fur.

Embrace imperfections

Remember that nature is imperfect, and your sketches should reflect its organic beauty. Don't be afraid to embrace imperfections and let go of expectations.

GO
birdwatching

Wherever we are in the world, we're likely accompanied by feathered friends, their birdsong a sound we've grown accustomed to. When we slow down, we notice just how many different species of birds there are. There's a real sense of accomplishment and excitement in learning about and observing birds in their natural habitat.

TIPS ON HOW TO BIRDWATCH

Choose your location. Habitats which attract a variety of birds are wooded areas, wetlands or open fields. That said, local parks, nature reserves and even your own backyard will have some feathered friends.

Get equipped

It's handy to have a field guide to local birds to help you to identify them, or you might prefer a bird ID app on your phone. If you want to take it up a notch, you could equip yourself with a set of binoculars, as well as a notebook and pen to record your observations.

Be patient

You'll want to find a quiet spot where you can sit comfortably. Listen out for birdsong and calls as you observe the toing and froing around you. Your field guide or app will help you with features such as feather patterns, markings, size and behaviours, which will aid in identifying the species. Note down the date, time, location, weather conditions and any species you've seen on your birdwatching walk.

Respect their environment

Be sure to take home any litter and to leave the area as undisturbed as possible. Remain a respectful distance away from the birds and never touch their nests.

SUPPORT YOUR
local birds

When you're out for a stroll, you can do more than just enjoy the scenery – you can also make a difference for the local bird population. Our feathery friends eat as much as half of their body weight in a single day. In winter, especially, it's difficult for them to get the sustenance they need – and by building roads, towns and cities, we've taken much of their habitat from them.

Making bird-feeder pine cones is a simple and enjoyable craft project that can provide essential food for local birds. Here's how to make them:

1. **Gather your supplies:** You'll need pine cones, birdseed, peanut butter (or other bird-safe sticky substance like suet or vegetable shortening), a butter knife or spatula, and string or twine. Bonus points if you collect pine cones while on a walk! Those that are closed-up tight will open up after a short blast in the microwave – 30 seconds should be enough.

2. **Attach the string:** Cut a length of string or twine, around 15–20 centimetres (6–8 inches) long, and tie it securely around the top of each pine cone. This will serve as the hanger for your bird feeder.

3. **Apply the peanut butter:** Melt the peanut butter and, using a butter knife or spatula, spread a generous layer over the entire surface of the pine cone. Make sure to apply the peanut butter into the crevices between the scales for maximum coverage.

4. **Roll in birdseed:** Roll the peanut butter-coated pine cone in the birdseed, pressing gently to ensure the seeds adhere to it, until the cone is completely covered.

5. **Hang them up:** Once the pine cone is fully coated with birdseed, hang it from a tree branch or another suitable spot, with a smile, knowing you've done your little bit for your local birdlife.

LEAVE PLACES AND SPACES BETTER THAN YOU FOUND THEM

Imagine what the world could be like if we all adopted the mentality of leaving things better than we found them. We've all been on walks where we've seen the hedgerows littered with debris – debris that's potentially deadly for wildlife habitats. We sometimes underestimate the impact our actions can have. By vowing to collect litter whenever possible on our walks, we can play a crucial role in protecting and preserving ecosystems.

Doing good does us good; acts of kindness create a "helper's high", as our brain releases all those feel-good endorphins which light up its pleasure centre.

Here are some things to consider:

You might need supplies

It's useful to carry a pair of sturdy gloves to protect your hands, particularly if the litter has any sharp rusty edges – always be cautious. Reusable bags minimize waste and environmental impact.

How you'll dispose of the waste

Once you've filled your bags with litter, properly dispose of the waste in designated receptacles or recycling bins.

The difference you're making

By removing litter from the environment, you have helped to prevent pollution and protect wildlife. Your actions make a difference, contributing to a cleaner, healthier planet.

TAKE GOOD CARE
OF THE PLANET

As we inhabit this planet, we'd be forgiven for thinking that in the grand scheme of things what we do makes little difference. However, our choices can and do impact the health and future of Earth.

Take, for instance, walking as a mode of transportation. It's less noisy and a zero-emission form of transport because it doesn't emit harmful air pollutants or greenhouse gases like vehicles do. When we opt to walk instead of driving, we're significantly reducing our carbon footprint.

On a personal and governmental level, walking requires minimal infrastructure and fewer resources compared with cars, buses or trains. All that's needed are pathways and pavements. Construction and maintenance costs are much lower, and we see less habitat destroyed to make way for all the roads, railways and fuel stations.

Our green spaces play a vitally important role in maintaining biodiversity, regulating local climates and providing recreational places for communities. Walking helps to preserve and protect green spaces, such as parks, forests and nature reserves, ensuring that these valuable ecosystems remain accessible and intact for future generations to enjoy.

Every step you take enhances the overall quality of life, not just for yourself, but for the planet and for generations to come.

ON LOSING OUR WAY

Life is much like a winding path through the wilderness, full of twists, turns and unexpected obstacles. There are times when we feel as though we've lost our way. Unfortunately, we're not given a roadmap of how to live life when we're born and so, instead, we have to find our own way.

You'll make mistakes – we all do – they're how we learn. In times of uncertainty, it's important to trust in ourselves and our

ability to navigate whatever challenges come our way. Trust, too, in the process, embrace the unknown, and have faith that you are exactly where you need to be.

It's important to remember that there is no one right path in life – only the right path for us – and that we're wiser than we give ourselves credit for. More than any other human being, we tend to know what's right and wrong for *us*. Sometimes, though, we lack the courage to forge our own path or align with our own personal values because we worry what other people may say or think. Always remember: this life of yours is *yours*. Yours to live and design and create how you see fit.

Happiness walks on busy feet.

KITTE TURMELL

With each step,

we can breathe in

possibility and exhale

our doubts and fears

LIFE LESSONS FROM NATURE

Nature has countless lessons to offer if we take the time to observe and listen. From the resilience of a tree weathering a storm to the intricate teamwork of a colony of ants, the natural world is rich with wisdom. Here are some key lessons we can learn from nature:

Rewilding is normal

Just as nature reclaims abandoned spaces, we too can rediscover our wild essence, reconnecting with the untamed parts of ourselves to find vitality and balance in a world of order and structure.

Expect ebbs and flows

Life, like the tide, offers moments of abundance and challenge. Embracing these natural rhythms allows us to navigate life's currents with grace and resilience.

Mighty things grow from humble beginnings

Just as mighty oaks grow from tiny acorns, small ideas have the potential to blossom into profound change. By nurturing even the smallest sparks of inspiration, we can cultivate a forest of innovation and possibility.

In the right environments, we thrive

Like plants seeking sunlight, we flourish when surrounded by supportive environments that nurture our growth and well-being. By cultivating spaces of positivity and encouragement, we create fertile soil for personal and collective transformation.

Growth and transformation take time

Just as seeds need time to germinate and grow, personal growth and transformation unfold gradually. By embracing patience and perseverance, we allow ourselves the space to evolve and bloom in our own time.

The balance of giving and receiving

In the intricate web of life, every action has a ripple effect. By giving back to our communities and the natural world, we contribute to a cycle of reciprocity and abundance, enriching both our own lives and the world around us.

Change is inevitable

Like the turning of the seasons, change is a constant and natural part of life. By embracing change with an open heart and a spirit of adaptability, we unlock the door to new opportunities and endless possibilities.

CONCLUSION

Walking isn't just about putting one foot in front of the other – it's a profound act of self-care, mindfulness and connectivity – changing lives in a variety of ways.

You'll start to feel itchy feet when you haven't been out for a while. There'll be a contrast between how you feel on the days you did go for a stroll and the days you didn't. Where once you may have felt stuck in your own head, there's a newfound appreciation for the environment and you'll feel attuned with the seasons. The best bit? Feeling healthier, happier and more connected to yourself than ever before.

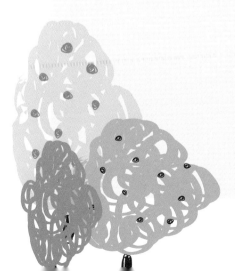

But perhaps most importantly, you've discovered that walking is a gift – a simple yet magnificent way to give back to yourself, to others and to the planet. It's a reminder that even amid life's challenges and uncertainties, there is always solace to be found in the simple act of putting one foot in front of the other.

So, as you step out into the world, may you carry with you the lessons learned from your walks – the importance of presence, gratitude and self-care. And may each journey be a reminder of the incredible gift of walking – for it is in motion that we find stillness, and in stillness that we find ourselves.

IMAGE CREDITS

GARDENING FOR MIND BODY AND SOUL

How to Nurture Your Well-Being with Nature

ISBN: 978-1-80007-162-9

Hardback

Gardening for Mind, Body and Soul will help you discover the joys and health-giving benefits of nurturing a garden.

We have long been aware of the positive effects of spending time in nature and how it can be a powerful antidote to the stresses of modern life. Science now tells us that cultivating a green space of our own can be restorative and even transformative for our physical and mental well-being, with a proven ability to reduce depression and anxiety, boost our happiness levels and provide a feeling of balance and calm.

Tips and Guided Exercises
to Help Overcome Trauma

AMANDA MARPLES

THE HEALING WORKBOOK

Tips and Guided Exercises to Help Overcome Trauma

ISBN: 978-1-80007-768-3

Paperback

The Healing Workbook contains practical advice, effective tips and guided exercises based on trusted cognitive behavioural therapy (CBT) techniques to help you begin the process of recovery. Within these pages you will find support and encouragement as you begin to come to terms with the past and find your way back to yourself, your values and a life where you can flourish and thrive.

Use the workbook either on its own or alongside therapy to help you work through your trauma and find a sense of peace and healing.

Have you enjoyed this book?

If so, why not write a review on
your favourite website?

If you're interested in finding out more about
our books, find us on Facebook at **Summersdale
Publishers**, on Twitter/X at **@Summersdale** and
on Instagram and TikTok at **@summersdalebooks**
and get in touch. We'd love to hear from you!

Thanks very much for buying
this Summersdale book.

www.summersdale.com